THE YOGURT BOOK

THE YOGURT BOOK
100 Ways to Use Yogurt Besides Eating It Out of a Container

Connie Berman
and
Susan Katz

GROSSET & DUNLAP
A FILMWAYS COMPANY
Publishers • New York

Acknowledgments

Thanks to Lenore Berg, James Blankenship, Roseann Hirsch, Susan Netter, and Maureen Sugden, and to our editor, Joyce Frommer, and our agent, Judi Ehrlich, for all their help and support. Thanks also to Marcella Berti, whose twinkling fingers typed till the wee hours of many mornings. And special thanks to Barney and Bob for eating all that yogurt.

Contents

INTRODUCTION

One clear and beautiful day in a small Turkish mountain village, a wizened old man was seen perched on a log at the shore of a peaceful lake. The man was both a sage and a scholar, but sometimes also considered a fool. Villagers watched in astonishment as the man, bent with age as he was, stirred spoonful after spoonful of yogurt into the lake. Even the small children of the village gathered around him, giggling at his strange actions. But the man paid them no mind. All day long he stirred and he stirred and he stirred. Finally, when dusk was settling upon the hills of the village, one of the townspeople, a prosperous merchant, approached the old man.

"Old man," said the merchant, "just what do you think you're doing?"

The old man answered quite earnestly, "I am trying, my friend, to make yogurt."

The crowd around the old man burst into the laughter they had been holding in all day.

The old man shook his head knowingly. "You laugh now," he said, "but just think how wonderful it would be if we could have a whole lakeful of yogurt."

This old Turkish legend has been cherished and passed down from generation to generation as has been their special yogurt culture. Yogurt has been a basic part of Turkish cuisine and history for hundreds of years.

And it dates back even farther than that. There are references to yogurt in the Bible; Homer sang its praises in the *Iliad;* and desert nomads packed their yogurt cultures, right along with their camels, wives, and tents, when they changed oases.

En route from the Middle East and antiquity to America in the twentieth century, yogurt went through a lot of changes. It started life as a simple fermented milk product and became, besides a nourishing food, a universal panacea for everything from baldness to impotence. By the time yogurt reached the States in the early part of the 1900s, its reputation as an elixir had so preceded it that the only people not scared off by its supposed miracle-working benefits were considered health fanatics. After all, the general public reasoned, could something so good for you possibly taste good? It has only been in the past two decades that Americans have discovered what the rest of the world has known for four thousand years—that yogurt tastes as good as it is good for you.

Yogurt *is* good for you! The sour milk culture with the tart, tangy taste has many healthful benefits that have been proven by medical research. Whether yogurt is truly an aphrodisiac, can make your hair grow, or erase wrinkles remains to be seen. But the power of positive thinking goes a long way in turning legend into fact.

What definitely is fact is that yogurt is more than just a container full of white stuff, and more than just a convenience food to be eaten on the run. An important food in maintaining good health, it's chock-full of proteins and vitamins. It's a versatile cooking ingredient, the basis of many exotic recipes and just as many everyday ones, from quiche to casserole. It's a remedy for a variety of ailments. It's an essential element in all kinds of homemade beauty preparations. Above all, it's a substance with a long and fascinating history that had its beginnings in the desert over four millennia ago.

100 WAYS TO USE YOGURT

1. Combine with chives instead of sour cream for baked potatoes.
2. Add to garlic sautéed in butter for a quick pasta sauce.
3. Mix with honey for a facial mask.
4. Use as a remedy for stomach upset.
5. Blend with onion-soup mix for a party dip.
6. Substitute for milk in soufflés and omelettes.
7. Whip with egg yolks to make deviled eggs.
8. Blend with tomato juice for a refreshing skin toner.
9. Use as a mouthwash for bad breath.
10. Add to pan drippings to make gravy.
11. Make yogurt Popsicles by freezing fruit-flavored yogurt in ice-cube trays. Use Popsicle sticks for handles.
12. Combine with chopped apple, raisins, and nuts for a quick sundae.
13. Mix with honey, eggs, and a dash of bourbon to make a yogurt eggnog. Sprinkle with nutmeg and cinnamon.
14. Combine with warm olive oil for a hair treatment.
15. Whip with egg whites for a dessert topping.
16. Take for relief from colitis.
17. Substitute for water in making gelatin desserts.
18. Make Turkish buttermilk by mixing 3 parts yogurt and 1 part water with a dash of salt.
19. Use as postsurgery nourishment.
20. Combine with ricotta cheese and use in lasagne.
21. Heat with Cheddar or Swiss cheese for a zesty cheese sauce.
22. Add to oatmeal to make a toning face wash.
23. Strain overnight in cheesecloth to make yogurt cream cheese.
24. Mix with tuna or minced clams for a cocktail dip.
25. Apply to face and leave on overnight as a face cream.
26. Use as a remedy for dysentery.
27. Make a frappé with canned fruit cocktail, grenadine, and yogurt, whipped together in a blender.
28. Add to dry cereal instead of milk.
29. Use in chocolate-cake mix for an extra-rich dessert.
30. Blend with a pureed avocado and use as a face conditioner.
31. Take for relief from rash and itch of allergies.
32. Substitute for mayonnaise in potato salad.
33. Feed to babies as an antidote to diarrhea.

34. Add to herbal shampoo for extra-rich moisturizing.
35. Combine with garlic and mustard for steak sauce.
36. Eat before going to sleep to cure insomnia.
37. Use as a marinade.
38. Eat to restore bacteria killed by antibiotics.
39. Substitute for sour cream in beef Stroganoff.
40. Mix with dried or fresh fruit for a delicious pie filling.
41. Use as a digestive aid.
42. Use to help erase wrinkles and lines on the face.
43. Combine with caviar for a dip.
44. Blend with crushed ice in a blender for a cold drink.
45. Add to chunks of Roquefort cheese for a salad dressing.
46. Mix with chili sauce and lemon juice for a seafood sauce.
47. Use as a sunburn cream.
48. Substitute for milk in pancake batter.
49. Eat to cure a hangover.
50. Add to coffee and brandy for a sauce over cake and ice cream.
51. Mix with herbs for a soothing lotion for the face.
52. Combine with brewer's yeast for a beauty mask.
53. Combine with tomato juice and spices for a "Yogurt Mary."
54. Take for relief from gassy, bloated feeling.
55. Use as a topping for borscht.
56. Blend with watercress in a blender to make a delicious dip.
57. Mix with water and use as a hair setting lotion.
58. Use as a laxative.
59. Combine with fresh fruit, club soda, and honey for a cocktail.
60. Substitute for sour cream in chicken paprikash.
61. Use as a soaking solution for fingernails to bleach out nicotine or cooking stains.
62. Use as a chaser for hot, spicy foods.
63. Add to curry sauce to better blend the spices.
64. Mix with almond meal for a face cleanser.
65. Eat to calm frazzled nerves.
66. Substitute for water or milk in making canned soups.
67. Take to prevent and cure fever blisters or cold sores.
68. Combine with frozen fruit-juice concentrate and vanilla flavoring, and freeze into sherbet.
69. Rub into hair to cure baldness.
70. Mix with lemon juice and use as an astringent.
71. Beat with an egg for a hair conditioner.

72. Blend with mayonnaise and pickle relish
to make tartar sauce.

73. Take instead of aspirin for relief from migraine headaches.

74. Mix with lactose-fermenting yeasts for a carbonated
alcoholic beverage.

75. Substitute for milk in instant-pudding mix.

76. Mix with chopped garlic and eat as
a preventative against malaria.

77. Use as a vaginal douche to combat yeast infections.

78. Substitute for mayonnaise in salad sandwiches.

79. Eat to prevent food poisoning when visiting
foreign countries.

80. Mix with papaya for a face freshener that
sloughs off dead skin.

81. Add to your favorite bottled salad dressing
to increase protein value.

82. Combine with Epsom salts for a footbath.

83. Use instead of antacid tablets to soothe ulcers.

84. Blend with equal part fruit (or vegetable) juice
for a refreshing drink.

85. Whip with fresh, pureed peach for a facial mask.

86. Thicken with flour, heat, and add a dash of Worcestershire
sauce to use over cooked green vegetables.

87. Add enough to almond meal to make an abrasive paste for
heels and elbows.

88. Apply to skin to bleach out freckles.

89. Reduce calories, by using it for a yogurt-only lunch.

90. Mix with a mashed banana for a facial for dry skin.

91. Freeze overnight in its container and take for a snack on a
long trip. It will defrost by the time you're ready to eat.

92. Combine with camomile tea and use
on face as a moisturizer.

93. Eat to achieve healthier skin and nails.

94. Add to chopped cabbage and chopped carrot for coleslaw.

95. Mix with baking soda or cornstarch and add to bath water.

96. When making meat loaf or meatballs,
use to moisten ingredients.

97. Blend with cooked barley for a toning facial.

98. Use it regularly on a low cholesterol diet.

99. Combine with peeled, finely chopped cucumber and some
chopped onion to make a sauce for fried fish.

100. Use instead of custard in a pie earmarked for throwing.

THE YOGURT BOOK

[1]

THE HISTORY OF YOGURT

It Started with a Goatskin Bag

Empires and hemlines have risen and fallen as the centuries have slipped by, but yogurt has endured through it all. Despite its recent surge in popularity in the United States, despite its so-called discovery by everyone in America from kids to grandmothers, the fact is that yogurt is over four thousand years old. The sour milk culture dates back to the days of antiquity. Even some of the earliest records are filled with notes about yogurt. There are varied references to it in early folkloric histories of such far-flung lands as Scandinavia, Mongolia, Lapland, and Iceland. While we in America have just begun to savor its tart taste and its many virtues, the people of eastern Europe have been enjoying yogurt and writing about its healthful benefits for thousands of years.

Yogurt existed in biblical times. The Old Testament depicts wise old Abraham, certainly well known for his longevity and his virility, partaking of goat's milk yogurt. Persian folklore further expands on Abraham and his diet of yogurt. According to legend, he was taught how to make the fermented milk stuff by an angel. The prophet Job, who patiently suffered through numerous trials and tribulations in his test of faith, referred to a milk curdled like cheese that he was served at an important meal.

No one knows exactly how yogurt was invented, or who was responsible for its discovery, but its origin is generally said to be in the Middle East, probably in the area known today as Turkey. According to the time-honored tale, yogurt came about through a serendipitous accident. A hungry nomad packed some milk away in a goatskin bag for sustenance while traveling on his camel across the desert. Many hours later, when the nomad opened up the bag to quench his thirst, he found that the milk had turned into a thick, tart custard. The heat of the sun and the motion of the bag against the camel's side, plus the bacteria on the inside of the goatskin bag, had produced perfect conditions for fermentation. And the result was yogurt. Hungry as he was, the nomad tasted the mixture and, delighted with its tangy flavor, quickly incorporated the new foodstuff into his diet. Yogurt fast became an important part of nomadic cooking.

There are some food historians, however, who say that yogurt dates back to an even earlier time. Reay Tannahill, author of several books on food, theorizes that yogurt and similar curdled milk products must have been discovered at about the beginning of the Neolithic era, when man first learned about milking. A container filled with milk, probably some sort of clay pot, was left outside for a period of time, perhaps temporarily forgotten. The milk fermented to form yogurt—what may be history's happiest accident.

In countries other than Turkey, ancient peoples were discovering the joys of yogurt, too. It was being consumed with gusto in the Arab countries, Africa, the Balkans, central Asia, and southern Europe.

Tomes many centuries old sing the praise of yogurt and hail it as a miracle food, a cure-all that can purge the soul of evil spirits and cleanse the body. Whether these claims were substantiated or not, yogurt kept its reputation as a truly wondrous food.

The Greek historian Herodotus, who lived sometime during the fifth century B.C., wrote about yogurt. And Marco Polo described how the Mongolians boiled their milk and allowed it to curdle to make yogurt.

The Roman scholar Pliny the Elder called it nothing less than a divine food and a miracle milk. He wrote how the Persian women massaged their faces with yogurt to keep wrinkles and lines away.

In India, as far back as twenty-five hundred years ago, yogurt—as well as honey—was considered a food of the gods. All sour milk foods were absolutely forbidden to the devout and ascetic yogis—with the exception of *dahi,* the Indian version of yogurt. For the Indians who led a less restricted life and indulged in alcoholic beverages from time to time, yogurt was said to be an effective hangover cure. It was also helpful, Indians thought, in calming frazzled, jittery nerves and in preventing insomnia. Long before the world had invented Valium and Librium, the Indians had discovered their own nondrug tranquilizers.

Mahatma Gandhi, the late ruler of modern India, was also aware of the advantages of yogurt. Gandhi was very concerned with finding effective ways to feed the huge populations of his country. He wrote an insightful book on nutrition, called *Diet Reform,* in which he discussed yogurt and hailed it as a protein-filled, inexpensive food that could be eaten by the poor to foster good health.

In ancient Persia, yogurt played an important role in marriage arrangements. The worth of a woman ready for the altar was computed in terms of how much yogurt—or *mast,* as the Persians called the thick custard—her bridegroom could buy with her dowry.

The ferocious Mongolian conqueror Genghis Khan thrived on yogurt made from the milk of yaks and ewes. He fed it to his army to strengthen them for battle, and used it as a marinade to preserve meat while traveling with his troops.

Galen, a Greek physician and writer on medicine in the first century A.D., claimed that yogurt was "very beneficial for the bilious and burning stomach."

Dioscorides, another Greek physician prominent around A.D. 50 recommended yogurt for the liver, stomach, and the blood.

A thirteenth-century Persian historian named Lemgo wrote that an area of the Shah's palace was specially designated for the making of yogurt and other fermented milk products. This yogurt room in the palace was called Yoghurt Choeneck. Obviously, yogurt was a highly respected part of Persian cuisine.

The natives of the Middle East and Asia—the Mongolians, the Armenians, the Arabs, the Persians, the Bulgarians—had been making yogurt for centuries before the rest of western Europe finally caught on to its value. But once a country found out about the sour milk custard, it quickly made a place for itself at the dining table.

A Royal Remedy

Emperor Francis I learned about yogurt the hard way. The aged ruler of France during the sixteenth century was on his sickbed. His strength was slipping away and his health was becoming worse by the hour. None of his esteemed court physicians could help him. It appeared that the emperor was doomed. There seemed to be nothing anyone could do.

Then the emperor learned of a healer from Constantinople, who was said to cause miracles with his secret-formula cures. Some of the emperor's guards were immediately dispatched to bring the healer to the court. The healer—an ancient, bearded Jew—arrived and prepared his magic potion for the emperor, in exchange for an exorbitant fee of thousands of francs. His so-called secret formula was actually just plain yogurt prepared from goat's milk.

When the emperor, as the legend goes, began eating the yogurt, his health and vitality returned to him. After a few days, he was well enough to leave his sickbed, to which he had been confined for months. Soon, he no longer felt ill and listless, but rejuvenated with new vigor and fortitude.

Francis I did not care that he had paid a small fortune for his cure; he was, after all, a new man. He became so enamored of this secret formula, which he felt had saved his life, that he thereafter respectfully called it *le lait de vie eternelle*—the milk of eternal life.

The Man Who Wanted to Live Forever

The man who was most responsible for taking yogurt out of the nomad's goatskin bag and putting it onto the twentieth-century kitchen table was a Russian scientist named Ilya Metchnikoff. Like many men, Metchnikoff wanted to live as long as he could, at least to be a hundred.

Metchnikoff had won the coveted Nobel Prize, in 1908, for his work on the way white blood cells help fight infection and disease. Through his research, he had become very conscious of how illness ravages the body, of how the aging process deteriorates the organs. Metchnikoff didn't want that to happen to him. He delved deeply into all the books and studies he could find on longevity and aging, hoping to find the answer to long life.

In the course of his detailed research, the Russian scientist discovered something important about the Bulgarians. In a turn-of-the-century report, they were stated to have a high rate of people living to be one hundred or older. The report said that out of every thousand deaths, an average of four were people who had passed the century mark. The average Bulgarian lived to be eighty-seven, as compared to the much lower average life expectancy found in other countries, including the United States. Since the Bulgarians consumed yogurt voraciously, as much as six pounds daily in some instances, Metchnikoff concluded that yogurt was responsible for such longevity.

He then set about to analyze the composition of yogurt and to isolate the bacteria in it which contributed to its healthful effects. Under a powerful microscope, the scientist, who was then director of the Pasteur Institute in Paris, discovered rod-shaped creatures swimming around in the yogurt culture. Metchnikoff called these *Lactobacillus bulgaricus.*

These bacteria, Metchnikoff believed, were the key to good health. They were the miracle workers that would chase the "wild, poisonous and putrefying bacteria out of the large intestine."

It was the large intestine, Metchnikoff theorized, that was the root of all evil in man. He felt that all the destructive and toxic bacteria in the body gathered there to wreak dire damage on the system. His thoughts about the large intestine were so radical that he even urged the possibility of surgical removal. He felt that this surgery would prevent the poisoning of the body. For those who would (wisely) shun such treatment, Metchnikoff advocated eating yogurt. The *Lactobacillus bulgaricus* in yogurt—the friendly, beneficial bacteria— would prevail in the large intestine and keep out the harmful bacteria. Thus, Metchnikoff believed, yogurt would make for better health and a longer life.

In his book *The Prolongation of Life,* Metchnikoff expounded his theories on aging, longevity, and yogurt, which he regarded as a miraculous, health-giving food. He himself practiced what he preached. The scientist consumed quarts of yogurt daily.

But unfortunately, Metchnikoff's theories about yogurt as the elixir of life have never been medically proven. He himself is not good testimony to his beliefs. He died in 1916, at the modest age of seventy-one—almost thirty years shy of the century mark that was his goal—despite the fact that he had been devouring yogurt religiously for twenty years.

Yogurt Crosses the Ocean and Becomes Big Business

While Metchnikoff was busy working on his theories about yogurt and longevity, a businessman named Isaac Carasso was busy manufacturing the cultured milk product in Spain. Carasso imported cultures from Bulgaria and the Pasteur Institute in France. At first, he marketed his yogurt through pharmacies. Then, in 1929, he expanded his business to France, establishing the Danone Company, named in honor of his son Daniel.

Carasso called his product the "Dessert of Happy Digestion." Whether that euphoric-sounding name was responsible or not, Carasso's sales continued to increase as more and more western Europeans became acquainted with the wonders of yogurt. (Today, the Danone Company, located in a large plant outside Paris, is one of the leading producers of yogurt in western Europe.) Even the food-snobbish French decided that yogurt was a dish to be savored by the most discriminating of gourmet palates.

At the onset of World War II, Carasso died, and the business was carried on by his son Daniel, who decided that it was time for yogurt to go to America. With his family, he emigrated to New York. On the way over to the United States from France, the young entrepreneur stopped in Spain to see the Metzgers, some old family friends. As the families were saying their farewells, Daniel Carasso urged the Metzgers to move to the United States, where they could all make yogurt.

The Metzgers followed up on Daniel's suggestion, and arrived in the New World about a year after Carasso and his family. With Carasso, the Metzgers, father and son, bought a New York factory in The Bronx that had already been supplying yogurt to the Turks, Greeks, and Arabs in the area. These immigrant groups still wanted to indulge their ethnic tastes and were eager to buy yogurt.

The factory produced a mere two hundred or so containers of yogurt a day, packaged in bottles. It was a simple, modest operation, with Juan, the younger Metzger, even going to work rinsing out the equipment. With the Carasso-Metzger takeover, the company was named Dannon. The name *Danone* had been Americanized. Thus, in 1942, one of the biggest and most successful yogurt companies was born.

After World War II ended, Carasso returned to France to concentrate on his yogurt business there, and the Metzgers became the heads of the Dannon Yogurt Company.

The success of Dannon was due to shrewd thinking on the part of the Metzgers. They were aware of the then nearly universal aversion to health foods and the commonly held belief that what was supposedly good for you couldn't possibly taste good. So the Metzgers did not tout their product as a health food but rather as a treat that was delicious.

Nevertheless, yogurt had such a strong image as a miracle-working food that could make for instant strength and health, as well as virility and longevity, that it had become the butt of satire. Jokes about yogurt abounded, like ones about one-hundred-year-old women eating yogurt and giving birth.

The Metzgers capitalized on this and also dabbled in humor to sell their product to a public suspicious of yogurt. The Dannon advertising campaigns played down the health-food aspect of yogurt and said it was not a miracle food that could help you lower your golf score. What yogurt was, they declared, was a snack that was really good.

The Metzgers also realized that one of the problems with yogurt, for the majority of Americans weaned on sweets and sugar-filled goodies, was its tart taste. To the yogurt novice, it tasted sour. So, in 1946, the first fruit-flavored Dannon was introduced. It was a strawberry yogurt—a few gobs of preserves had been put on the bottom of the container and plain yogurt added on top. This came to be known as sundae-style yogurt, because the preserves and the yogurt are separate (unmixed) until the yogurt eater blends the two together with a spoon. Then, voilà! Flavored yogurt!

In Swiss-style yogurt (a later development), the preserves and yogurt are already combined, but generally this variety has preservatives and other additives to maintain the texture. Western-style yogurt also has fruit, on the bottom, but there is the added bonus of a flavored-syrup topping on the plain yogurt.

Actually, Dannon was not the first company to produce flavored yogurt. A fruit yogurt had been introduced in Prague, Czechoslovakia, in 1933.

And Dannon was not the first company to peddle its sour milk product to Americans. The very first yogurt dairy in the United States had been established in Andover, Massachusetts, in 1931, by an Armenian family. They were the Columbosians, and with typical family pride, called their product Colombo.

In New York, a Greek family had founded the Oxygala Yogurt Company in The Bronx in 1932. *Oxygala* is the Greek word for sour milk, but perhaps the name was too unwieldly for American consumers, used to buying brands called simply Kraft or Borden's. Oxygala changed its name to Lacto.

Other companies took up yogurt making, like Dr. Gaymont in Chicago and Johnston's in the West. As yogurt caught on, and the health-food craze permeated down to the Cheerios-gulping masses, many dairy businesses began developing their own lines of yogurt.

Yogurt in Canadian Mountie Country

At about the same time that Daniel Carasso was setting up yogurt cultures in his Bronx factory, yogurt was also infiltrating America through its northern border. A group of Trappist monks came from Spain to settle in Canada. One of their traveling companions was a cow, brought along to provide milk for them during the long and tedious journey. From the milk furnished by the cow, the monks made yogurt.

Once they arrived in North America, the monks established a monastery in La Trappe, Quebec, where they actively pursued studies of health and nutrition, much of which focused on yogurt. The Oka Agricultural School was founded on the grounds of the monastery. Then, in 1932, the Rosell Bacteriological Dairy Institute, affiliated with the University of Montreal, was founded by Dr. José Rosell and Professor Gustave Toupin, at the La Trappe Monastery. There studies were made of the various fermented milk products, and the yogurt cultures were perfected, until today, as deemed by many yogurt aficionados, the culture from the Rosell Institute is the finest in the world.

In 1939, the outstanding yogurt culture produced by Rosell was permitted to be distributed in the United States. A Chicago businessman named Richard Tille then formed the Continental Yogurt Company; through a franchise, it used the Rosell cultures to produce commercial yogurt and also sold the culture mix for do-it-yourself-at-home yogurt. Then, in 1942, Tille moved to Los Angeles and established the Yami Yogurt Company, which also relied on the Rosell culture for yogurt production.

Yogurt Today

Yogurt, for so long stigmatized by its classification as a health food, its ethnic history, and its foreign-sounding name, has experienced a terrific explosion of popularity in the past few years. It has become one of the fastest-growing convenience foods ever, with U.S. sales skyrocketing from 17 million pounds in 1955 to 415 million pounds in 1975. The 1960s served as a catalyst to push yogurt into the mainstream of American diets. With the back-to-nature movement and renewed health consciousness, many Americans turned away from their starches and sugars, their gravy-laden red meats and other artery-hardening foods, and became more involved with foods that not only were delicious but also were nutritious. With a little experimentation, most people found that yogurt could be delicious, especially when souped up with fruit or bedazzled with honey and cinnamon. Not to mention its inclusion in gourmet treats such as soup, beverages, main dishes, and breads.

It is ironic that it took America so long to discover the food that Middle Easterners have been lapping up and loving for years, in fact, centuries. It is doubly ironic that Americans looked askance at this healthful food, which was, after all, "sour" and filled with bacteria. But once they approached for a taste, with more than a little trepidation, lured by a spoonful of preserves here and a dab of sugar there, Americans found that yogurt was wonderful. The food of the nomads has arrived in the United States and is here to stay.

[2]

YOGURT AND NUTRITION

Little Miss Muffet sat on a tuffet, eating her yogurt. Along came a spider, sat down beside her, and frightened Miss Muffet away.

Admittedly, that doesn't make for much of a rhyme, but it does make for the truth. Curds and whey is what the British used to call what we know today as yogurt.

Curd, by the way, is the stuff that separates from milk in a thick mass when acidic action occurs. Whey is the watery part of the separation, caused by the same process. They're both slightly acidic in taste, and are the results of milk curdling—in other words, yogurt.

Milk is probably the closest thing there is to a perfect food. So, since yogurt is made from milk, it follows only naturally that yogurt is almost as perfect as milk is, if not more so. As a matter of fact, yogurt has a bit more food value than milk. Because of the fermentation process—which turns the milk sugar into either lactic acid, gas or alcohol depending upon the kind of milk and/or method used—there is less sugar in yogurt than in milk. It is slightly higher in riboflavin and niacin, and the bacteria in yogurt more easily synthesize the vitamins in milk, making them more readily available to the system.

What Exactly Is Yogurt?

It is simply a milk product that, through the introduction of certain bacteria, has been fermented, cultured, or soured. It is similar, in that way, to sour cream or buttermilk—two other fermented milk products—but it is the specific bacteria introduced into warm milk, as well as the fact that these bacteria can and do thrive and multiply at close to body temperatures and above, that give yogurt its distinct qualities.

Two bacilli, *Lactobacillus bulgaricus* (remember Metchnikoff's studies?) and *Streptococcus thermophilus,* change the flavor of the milk from sweet to tart, produce the custardy consistency, and change the lactose (milk sugar) into lactic acid. Sometimes, other strains of bacteria, *acidophilus,* for example, are also added; in some areas, such as parts of the Middle East, Scandinavia, the Carpathians, and South America, lactose-fermenting yeasts are also present, resulting in yogurt that can be anywhere from slightly to potently alcoholic.

The bacteria are capable of living happily and multiplying profusely at certain temperatures—from 90°F. (a little below body temperature of 98.6°F.) to about 120°F.—and as they do, they cause the milk to ferment. (Other bacteria, such as those in sour cream and buttermilk, cannot survive above 90°F.) As a result of the acid formation, the proteins in milk are curdled, and the milk becomes yogurt.

The exact nutritional differences between different kinds of cow's milk (all of which make delicious yogurt) and yogurt can be seen from the chart on the next page.

(Per 8-oz. cup)	MILK				YOGURT	
	Whole	Skim	Evaporated (undiluted)	Condensed, Sweetened (undiluted)	Whole Milk	Skim
Water (%)	87	90	74	26	87	89
Calories	165	90	35	985	150	120
Protein (g.)	9	9	18	25	9	8
Fat (g.)	10	trace	20	25	7	4
Carbohydrates (g.)	12	13	24	170	12	13
Calcium (mg.)	285	298	635	829	280	295
Iron (mg.)	0.1	0.1	0.3	0.3	0.1	0.1
Vitamin A (I.U.)	390	170	820	1020	390	170
Thiamine (B^1) (mg.)	0.08	0.10	0.10	0.24	0.08	0.09
Riboflavin (B^2) (mg.)	0.42	0.44	0.84	1.21	0.42	0.43
Ascorbic acid (mg.)	2	2	3	3	2	2
Niacin (% of U.S. RDA)	trace	trace	trace	trace	trace	trace

Source: U.S. Department of Agriculture Yearbook of Nutritional Equivalents, 1959

When you add flavorings to yogurt, the calories go up appreciably, but the nutritional value stays exactly the same. The calorie differences between plain yogurt and different fruit-flavored yogurts can be seen here.

Calories per 8-oz. cup

Plain 120–150	Lemon 215	Peach melba 245
Apricot 204	Lime 210	Pineapple 235
Black cherry 230	Mandarin orange 225	Red raspberry 220
Blueberry 230	Peach 250	Strawberry 225

Another nutritional variable in yogurt is the type of milk it's made with. Cow's milk has the highest percentage of water; goat's milk has more calcium and vitamin A, and is more easily digestible because its fat globules are smaller. Mare's milk has twice as much vitamin C as human milk and four times as much as cow's milk. Reindeer milk has the greatest percentage of protein and fat; water buffalo's milk is high in lactose.

This is not to say that you should run out and try to get some kind of milk that you don't normally use. Some of the more exotic milks may not be your cup of yogurt. For example, goat's milk is extremely rich, very high in butterfat, and it makes some people ill. It can also be a vehicle for a germ that causes chronic brucellosis—a rare, but debilitating, stomach disease.

Besides the source of the milk, the type of grazing the animal does, what it's fed, and how and when it's milked can all affect the nutritional makeup of the milk, and subsequently, the yogurt.

One of the main reasons yogurt is often considered superior to milk is that before it reaches the consumer, milk is pasteurized at a high temperature, cooled, and then poured into sterile containers. This process kills germs and bacteria, which guarantees you can drink it without getting sick, but it also kills most of the vitamins and nutrients (that's why milk is often fortified with vitamin D). The bacterial cultures introduced by the yogurt activate the proteins and vitamins in milk that the sterilization process destroys. That's why, if you buy yogurt that has been pasteurized *after* it's been cultured (all yogurt is made with pasteurized milk to begin with; that's okay, since what the culturing does is reintroduce the "friendly," or beneficial, bacteria into the milk), it will still taste like yogurt, but all the beneficial bacteria will be dead and gone.

Most commercial yogurts are made from partially skimmed milk with instant nonfat milk powder added to thicken them. Some companies add dextrose for a sweeter-tasting yogurt; others add carrageen as a thickener. Fortunately or unfortunately, depending on how you look at it, the Food and Drug Administration has no "standard of identity" for yogurt, so all ingredients must be listed on the container. What this means, though, is that even if the bacteria are no longer alive (because of postculturing pasteurization) or if there are additives that might deactivate the yogurt, what you get is still called yogurt, even if, technically, it isn't.

Another reason yogurt rates above milk is that it takes the digestive system three to four hours to break down the sugars in milk. Since yogurt is "predigested" by its bacteria, it takes only one hour for 90 percent of the yogurt to be assimilated into the body. It can therefore be easily digested by the elderly and the very young, both of whom have delicate digestive systems; and often by people who suffer from lactose intolerance. (People who have this problem, genetically lack the enzyme necessary to break milk sugar down into lactic acid, and, therefore, cannot digest milk.)

During the culturing process—those hours when the culture is growing in a warm, undisturbed atmosphere—the biological value of protein in milk increases. And since the proteins in milk are believed to stimulate hepatic and intestinal secretions, and since, also, yogurt works to increase these stimulations by activating protein, the value of yogurt in the digestive system is even greater than that of milk. Also, the bacteria convert the lactose in milk to lactic acid, a digestive antiseptic. You get a little alcohol and a little carbonic acid, which act like a tonic to the nerves of the intestinal tract.

What else does yogurt do to make it so good for you? It can enhance the usefulness of some minerals, like calcium and phosphorus (necessary for the development of strong bones and teeth), by making them more readily available for absorption. Vitamins, especially the B complex, are said to be synthesized by the bacteria in yogurt. As a result, there may be an increase in folic and folinic acids, components of the B vitamins especially important in preventing anemia and nutritional deficiencies.

And one more thing, yogurt can also hinder the growth, or kill, some pathogenic organisms. Dysentery bacteria, for example, cannot live and develop in an acid medium; neither can *Salmonella typhi,* the bacteria that cause salmonella. Other harmful bacteria can't develop or are inhibited by the bacterial and acidic content of yogurt.

With all these benefits, it might be hard to believe that yogurt isn't *the* perfect food. It isn't. It's deficient in iron, copper, and vitamin C; it's lower in fat and vitamin A than milk (because, commercially, it's made from skimmed milk with nonfat milk solids added); it's not, nor is milk, for that matter, nearly as good a source of protein as meat or fish. But don't lose heart. There is no perfect food, and yogurt's beneficial qualities make it part of a healthy, balanced diet.

The differences between yogurt and other fermented milk products—sour cream, buttermilk, acidophilus milk, and kefir—are nutritional, "cultural," and a matter of taste.

Yogurt has a higher percentage of lactic acid than other fermented milks, and it's richer in the vitamin-B complex. A combination of bacteria is used in the culturing process, different from the ones used to make sour cream or buttermilk; the fermentation process for yogurt requires several hours at a relatively high heat, which would kill the strains of bacteria in the others. Kefir is cultured with bacteria and lactose-fermenting yeasts; acidophilus milk comes from the lactic fermentation of milk with the pure culture of *Lactobacillus acidophilus* (which is available in yogurt form in health-food stores). Acidophilus milk can be incubated like yogurt because some strains will curdle milk in a few hours at high temperatures. Both buttermilk and sour cream are cultured at room temperature for twenty to twenty-four hours.

In terms of taste and consistency, yogurt is eaten as a custard rather than drunk as a liquid; it has a firm curd, smooth and fine texture, and solid body. Buttermilk curd is soft and fragile, churned into a thick liquid. There is little or no alcohol in most yogurt, and the acid content is quite high. Kefir, in comparison, is alcoholic and self-carbonating, with one percent lactic acid, one percent alcohol. Acidophilus is generally sold as milk; its taste is a difficult one for people to enjoy, so it is usually masked by adding fruit juice or honey. There is currently a "sweet" acidophilus milk on the market (artificially sweetened), thought to be the answer for people with lactose intolerance, but its value is being hotly debated by nutritionists and health-food fans.

The slightly tart taste of yogurt, was the root of its dislike. People thought it was spoiled milk and wouldn't go near it. Yogurt does become more acidic and tarter as it gets older, but it is not stale and certainly not harmful to eat after the expiration date on the container. Yogurt does lose its beneficial bacteriological value after a month or so. In comparison, if ordinary milk sours, it should *not* be used—the bacteria could be dangerous, and the taste and smell are definitely unpleasant.

If you should choose to buy yogurt rather than make your own, be aware of the different styles as well as brands. Plain yogurt, from either whole or low-fat milk, is available pasteurized before or after the culture has been added. As we mentioned before, yogurt is a "living" food, and you'll miss out on its real benefits if you buy it as a nonliving culture.

Flavored yogurt comes in two basic forms: sundae-style, with the preserves on the bottom to be stirred into the plain yogurt by the consumer; and Swiss-style, with the preserves premixed by the man-ufacturer. Purists claim that not only is the Swiss-style yogurt gummy and unattractive—it's homogenized, to distribute the flavoring evenly—but it often has artificial additives and inactive bacteria. No brand of Swiss-style yogurt is without some sort of additive, whether it's natural (like starch, pectin, gelatin, or caramel), to hold the fruit in suspension, or artificial (like potassium sorbate), for longer shelf life.

There is a third style of yogurt, available mostly in the western part of the country, that has preserves on the bottom and syrup on the top. The only advantage it seems to have is extra sweetness—but of course this means extra calories.

However you like your yogurt—plain or flavored, homemade or store bought—it's a nutritionally balanced food that can be beneficial in many ways.

[3]

YOGURT AND HEALTH

Since time immemorial, when yogurt was first discovered in that nomad's leather bag, the sour milk culture has been considered a miracle food. Claims for its wondrous effects in curing diseases are as widespread and as encyclopedic as a medical dictionary of ailments. Yogurt, declare its passionate devotees, can cure everything from impotence to thinning hair and hangovers. For just about any disease or malady you can name, you can be sure that somewhere there's a yogurt aficionado who swears that the fermented milk product is the perfect antidote. To the staunchest of the yogurtophiles, it is a culinary faith healer, an indisputable miracle-working food that is the answer to all your problems, physical as well as spiritual.

The truth, of course, lies somewhere in between the miraculous and the medically proven. Yogurt is not a magic food—if you ate yogurt only, and no other foods, you would not be able to survive well or maintain a decent standard of good health.

But if you integrate yogurt into your diet, supplemented by other healthful and nutritious foods, you'll be farther along the way to maintaining good health than a person who stays away from the sour-tasting custard.

Among the benefits attributed to yogurt by its most ardent advocates are that it prolongs youth and life, can make a person more beautiful or handsome, fortifies the soul, stabilizes weight and paves the way for gain or loss as needed, restores thinning hair, and increases sexual prowess. None of these claims has ever been medically proven. Certainly it would be difficult to determine, using scientific methods, just how much yogurt fortifies the soul. But the power of suggestion is mighty, and if a yogurt lover believes that it will help his balding scalp, perhaps it just might do so.

According to various theorists, yogurt has been used successfully in connection with the following diseases and ailments: arthritis, hepatitis, migraine headaches, constipation, diarrhea, dysentery, flatulence, kidney maladies, cholera, colitis, gallstones, bad breath, skin diseases, typhoid fever, arteriosclerosis, sunburn, allergies, vaginal infections, infantile gastroenteritis, and stomach ulcers.

The ways in which yogurt has been used medically are vast and varied. But what is the real story? What can yogurt do and what can't it do? What do medical researchers and doctors say about yogurt and health?

Yogurt and Antibiotics

Yogurt has been shown, according to medical research, to combat positively the adverse effects of antibiotics on the system. Such germ-killing drugs as penicillin, streptomycin, Aureomycin, and tetracycline, destroy the harmful bacteria that cause infection, but they also kill the beneficial bacteria in the intestine. The intestinal flora, as these bacteria are called, are vital to good elimination. When these bacteria are killed, fungus and mold spring up in their place, invading the intestine and even spreading to other organs.

By eating yogurt at every meal, a person on antibiotics can restore these missing microorganisms to his body within thirty-six to forty-eight hours. An eight-ounce container of yogurt can successfully counteract the harmful antibiotic effect of fourteen units of penicillin.

Intestinal Problems

The intestinal flora are considered by many doctors and health-wise laymen to be the key to good health. And that good health arises when there is a predominance of friendly, or beneficial, bacteria over harmful bacteria known as *B. coli.* The large intestine, about five to six feet long, is inhabited by trillions of bacteria. The idea behind a well-balanced diet is to eat those kinds of foods that will help establish the prevalence of beneficial bacteria over harmful bacteria.

Studies of yogurt have shown that the simple cultured milk product can do just that. The result is that intestinal ailments, like constipation, diarrhea, indigestion, and queasiness—all of which cause a lack of energy which may, in turn, lead to depression—can be alleviated and even prevented by eating yogurt.

Dr. Harry Seneca, of the Columbia University College of Physicians and Surgeons, found, through his detailed study of the effects of yogurt, that yogurt is a nutritional approach to the effective management of intestinal problems. His research also confirmed that yogurt definitely restores the intestinal flora, which in turn, will counteract the harmful effects of antibiotics on the intestines.

Research undertaken by three American scientists has demonstrated that yogurt killed eighteen types of harmful bacteria, including those which cause dysentery and pneumonia.

And a Turkish study on the bacterial value of yogurt showed that it destroys two types of human tuberculosis bacilli and one type of bovine tuberculosis bacilli.

As a matter of fact, way before modern research on yogurt began, physicians in seventh-century Greece, Syria, Arabia, Persia, and India were recommending yogurt for soothing and regulating the digestive tract. They felt that yogurt strengthened the stomach and made it impervious to illness.

Inhabitants of the Balkans also believe it is an effective cure for intestinal ailments, including constipation, colitis, and ulcers.

Yogurt and Senior Citizens

Yogurt is especially good for elderly people. Many of our older citizens develop digestive disorders because of a lack of hydrochloric acid in their stomachs. Hydrochloric acid is important because it aids in the digestion of proteins and vitamin C. Yogurt counteracts this deficiency and makes for more efficient digestion.

Yogurt is also good for older people because it can be digested more quickly and easily than its sister product, milk. Dr. Dick Kleyn, of Rutgers University, discovered in his yogurt studies that this is because the protein in yogurt is already partially broken down during its manufacture.

It would seem the more time an undigested food remains in the stomach and digestive tract, the more likelihood of conflict—the result of which is indigestion. Easily digested, yogurt is also recommended for postsurgery patients.

Yogurt has also been shown to be effective in combating constipation and irregularity, especially in older people. Research by Dr. Francis P. Ferrer and Dr. Linn J. Boyd, of New York Medical College, demonstrated that Dannon's Prune Whip yogurt was helpful in treating geriatric patients who complained of constipation and diabetic ulcers. When taken every night, prune whip yogurt (which was developed especially for treatment of constipation), was effective in more than 95 percent of the cases tested among these older patients.

Yogurt and Children

At the other end of the age spectrum are babies and young children, who have problems with diarrhea and with digesting some foods. Yogurt was found to be more effective in treating children's diarrhea than commercial preparations such as Kaopectate. Regular intake of yogurt by babies and children can also serve to prevent the growth of undesirable bacteria that cause diarrhea. Of course, if your child or infant is ill you should always consult your family physician.

Stomach Upset

Yogurt provides relief from stomach upset. Some people claim that when a queasy, unsteady feeling hits their stomachs, yogurt is the only food that they find palatable. Even when the sight or idea of any other substance makes their stomachs heave and lurch, they can eat yogurt. It settles the stomach and quells the unsteady feeling.

Yogurt for People Who Can't Drink Milk

Those people who suffer from lactose intolerance often turn to yogurt to get the protein and calcium nutrients their bodies require. Lactose intolerance is an enzyme deficiency of a genetic nature, where lactase, the enzyme that breaks down the lactose in milk and paves the way for its digestion, is missing. When a lactose-intolerant person drinks milk or eats ice cream, he suffers from diarrhea, abdominal pains and cramps, and a gassy, bloated feeling.

Yogurt, however, is very low in lactose, and therefore can be digested more easily. In extreme cases of lactose intolerance, even yogurt may not be digested comfortably, since a product with any amount of lactose, no matter how little, can cause distress.

Yogurt and Adelle Davis

Famed nutritionist Adelle Davis extolled yogurt as a nearly perfect food. She found it to be an excellent source of protein and a safeguard against deficiencies of vitamins B and D, and calcium. Davis hailed yogurt as nutritionally superior to milk because of its easy digestion and because the beneficial bacteria could live at body temperature.

Davis believed that a person who lived on a diet completely lacking in B vitamins could get this complex by eating yogurt. This was so, she said, because the yogurt bacteria helps the growth of friendly bacteria in the intestine, which in turn manufacture B vitamins.

However, this claim has been disputed by Drs. K. M. Acott and T. P. Labuza of the University of Minnesota Department of Food Science and Nutrition. They assert that their research shows that yogurt bacteria actually use vitamin B and do not supply or help manufacture B vitamins.

Adelle Davis also recommended that travelers going to foreign countries would do well to eat large quantities of yogurt, starting about three weeks before the voyage. She felt that this pre-journey ingestion of yogurt every day could help to prevent food poisoning and immunize travelers against bad food and water abroad.

Yet, in the continuing controversy over the medicinal values of yogurt, this claim too has been disputed. Some scientists and doctors say that such immunization against food poisoning is impossible, because the beneficial effects of yogurt cannot be stored up; it must be eaten daily to be worthwhile.

Yogurt and Longevity

Will eating yogurt make you live to be a hundred years old? Yogurt has long been linked with longevity, even before Metchnikoff proposed this connection. Those yogurt-eating peoples who have passed the century mark and still bound about with as much energy as teenagers, help to lend credence to this claim. So do census reports of some areas of Russia and Bulgaria, high in yogurt consumption, which show a large number of centenarians. A 1930 census report, for example, said that 160 out of every million Bulgarians were over a hundred years old. This statistic was compared to a similar report in the United States, where only 9 out of each million were over a hundred. Among those aged Bulgarians, by the way, the incidence of baldness and white hair was surprisingly low.

Unfortunately, yogurt has never been scientifically proven to be directly related to longevity. Because of its beneficial effect on the large intestine, in which it installs a majority of friendly bacteria, yogurt does help to retard putrefaction. And since putrefaction is what occurs in the process of aging, yogurt can be said to stave off aging and thus help you to live longer. But the operative words here are *can* and *help*. Eating yogurt is not a definite method of achieving long life. It won't insure that you live to be a hundred, but it will help you (that help should not be interpreted as a guarantee) live a better and longer life because it will improve your health and digestion. This is true, of course, provided that you exercise good care in other facets of your diet and general health regimen. If you consume large hero sandwiches with garlic-laden, fatty meats, drink three martinis a day, and smoke a carton of cigarettes a week, topping off all these indulgences with yogurt may save you from an upset stomach, but that's about all.

Yogurt and Your Weight

Yogurt is not an instant means to weight loss; it won't transform you into a svelte beauty if you're overweight, nor will it turn a skinny body into a well-shaped one. But yogurt can help you *regulate* your weight, and is therefore a boon to both overweight and underweight people.

The key to dieting with yogurt is the principle of substitution. Yogurt does not have a miracle ingredient that makes pounds melt away. If you eat a container of yogurt plus a high-calorie meal, rich in gravies and sauces and gooey sweet stuff, you won't lose an ounce. With the extra calories from yogurt, as a matter of fact, you may even gain some weight. Rather than just adding yogurt to your regular diet, substitute it for those foods particularly high in calories.

A dessert of yogurt, even the fruit-flavored kind that contains as much as 260 calories per cup, is far less fattening than an éclair with custard filling and chocolate icing, at a hefty 316 calories, or a slice of apple pie with 350 calories. Try plain yogurt instead of mayonnaise in your tuna-fish sandwich; it will add only 10 percent of the calories mayonnaise will. Or, instead of your customary sour cream on a baked potato, simply mix some chives or green onion with a few dollops of yogurt to save calories. Yogurt can be substituted for cream cheese, cottage cheese, milk, heavy cream—almost any dairy product.

Yogurt as a snack is far better—more nutritious, less fattening— than a bag of pretzels or a packet of cookies. It also has a high satiety quality, so that a container of yogurt makes you feel full and satisfied. Since snacking is often the downfall of the dieter, the yogurt-snack habit—as part of a well-balanced total diet program—is a good one to form.

Many people who go on diets tend to cut out many foods that are vital to good health. Yogurt, when integrated sensibly into a reducing plan, will provide essential vitamins and proteins, and help you lose weight. It certainly is no magic potion, but it could sway junk-food eaters away from the cookies, cake, chips, and pretzels. Yogurt can help you establish good eating habits, an important step in reaching and maintaining your desired weight.

Yogurt and Disease

Dr. Khem M. Shahani, of the University of Nebraska Department of Food Science and Nutrition, has executed various studies and a solid program of research on yogurt. Hoping to investigate the nutritional values of yogurt, Dr. Shahani isolated a natural antibiotic produced by *Lactobacillus bulgaricus,* one of the two organisms used in the preparation of the yogurt culture. Thus, Dr. Shahani theorized, through yogurt, a consumer may ingest a natural antibiotic that could provide resistance to disease and infection. In other words, it is possible that out of the billions of bacteria in a container of yogurt, an organism might exist which is a penicillin-type cure-all. Obviously, if this is so, much more extensive research is needed to investigate the matter and perhaps support some of the more far-flung claims for yogurt.

In the course of his studies, Shahani has also looked into the effect yogurt might have on cancer. He has reported some positive, although limited, results.

Yogurt and Vaginal Infections

Many women have reported successful results with external use of yogurt to cure vaginal infections. The yogurt can be used as a douche or directly applied to the genital area. The theory behind the use of yogurt is that it restores normal acidity and pH balance to the vagina. It is also helpful in combating yeast infections, often side effects of large doses of some antibiotics. An interesting note here is that a feminist who used yogurt as treatment on a woman in a self-help center was charged with practicing medicine without a license. She was later acquitted.

Yogurt and Allergies

No one is quite sure exactly what allergies are or how to treat them successfully. Yogurt may be a possible allergy relief remedy because of its calcium content. Recent studies have shown that calcium medication is helpful in reducing allergic reactions; yogurt is an excellent source of calcium, and certainly more fun to take for allergy relief than a pill.

Yogurt as a Natural Tranquilizer

Having trouble sleeping? Try a container of yogurt before bed; it is thought to help cure insomnia. This is because of its high calcium content, which helps to soothe nerves and calm jittery, tense muscles. Calcium tablets are readily given to people suffering from tension and anxiety, which are often the cause of insomnia and allergies. It would follow that a cup of yogurt could be a good antidote to a bad case of the butterflies, the sneezies, or the "I-can't-fall-asleeps."

Yogurt and Cholesterol

A substance in yogurt just might be the answer for people suffering from high cholesterol levels. Research conducted by Dr. George V. Mann, a professor at Vanderbilt University in Tennessee, seemed to indicate that there is some aspect of yogurt that helps to lower the cholesterol level in the blood by lowering the amount the body produces.

Dr. Mann determined this through a study of the diet of a group of African tribesmen. His original purpose was not to study yogurt but to test the effects of chemical additives used in ice cream, chocolate and mayonnaise, and other products. He divided his subjects into two groups. One group ate yogurt loaded with these additives; the other, yogurt without them. Both groups consumed large amounts of yogurt, since their regular diet usually consists of about a gallon a day of a fermented milk product almost identical to yogurt.

Surprisingly, tests of both groups showed that cholesterol levels had dropped. As a matter of fact, the more yogurt consumed, the greater the drop in the level of cholesterol in the blood. An ironic result, since yogurt is considered a high cholesterol food. Mann concluded that somehow, through the intake of yogurt, the body's production of cholesterol is diminished.

Mann suspected that the yogurt bacteria produces a fatty substance, like an acid, that blocks cholesterol production in the liver. Continuing studies in the United States have also supported this. However, the studies are tentative at this point. With more detailed and exhaustive research, yogurt could be shown to have a revolutionary effect on the treatment of people with heart disease aggravated by high cholesterol levels in the blood.

Yogurt and Fever Blisters and Canker Sores

Prevention magazine has reported that eating a certain kind of yogurt tablet, those containing *Lactobacillus acidophilus,* can help to combat those painful and ugly afflictions—fever blisters and canker sores. Fever blisters, also known as cold sores, appear on the lips or outside the mouth, and are caused by a virus. Canker sores usually turn up inside the mouth and are associated with allergies, emotional stress, local injury, or even menstruation. Both kinds of lesions occur more frequently in the cold and biting winter months, but they can also be triggered by too much sunbathing.

Regular intake of acidophilus yogurt tablets, which is made from milk containing acidophilus culture, has not only helped the unsightly fever blisters and canker sores disappear, it has also helped prevent them from recurring. Medical studies, initiated by Dr. Don J. Weekes of Peter Bent Brigham Hospital in Boston, have demonstrated that the odds are 9 to 1 in favor of this kind of tablet clearing up even the most troublesome of these lesions. If you'd rather eat yogurt itself than take tablets, you must eat, in large quantities daily, yogurt containing the live culture *Lactobacillus acidophilus.*

No one is quite sure why the acidophilus type of yogurt should have curative results with fever blisters and canker sores. But doctors suspect that the lactic acid produced by the bacteria, which is very powerful in killing undesirable bacteria, has something to do with it.

Is Yogurt for Everyone?

Are there any bad effects from yogurt? Can it ever be harmful? In general, the answer to both questions is no, but there are a few people for whom eating yogurt is definitely not a good idea. As we mentioned earlier, anyone with an extremely severe case of lactose intolerance will not be able to digest yogurt comfortably. Even the small amount of lactose in yogurt is too much.

Research undertaken by Dr. Ernest Beutler, at the City of Hope Medical Center in California, indicates that people who suffer from galactokinase deficiency should also stay away from yogurt. This is a disease where those afflicted lack the enzyme necessary to break down milk and related products into glucose. The disease is rare but treatable, and can be diagnosed at a very early age. If milk, cheese, yogurt, and other milk products are eliminated from the diet, cataracts, which result when the milk is not broken down completely, can be inhibited.

Commercial yogurts generally have higher levels of galactose than homemade yogurts because, skim-milk powder is often added to whole milk to make the yogurt thicker, or because fat-free yogurts (made with skim milk with most of the butterfat removed) are high in carbohydrates, therefore high in galactose. In purely whole milk yogurt, the galactose content is a little more than 14 percent. In yogurts made with skim milk, the content can be as high as 22 to 24 percent.

Related research at Johns Hopkins University demonstrated that twenty-six rats, on a diet of yogurt and nothing else, developed cataracts. The cause, according to the researchers, was the high galactose content in the yogurt. Interestingly enough, an effort to disprove these results was made by a science class at Andrew Jackson High School in Queens, New York. Their rats, also fed a diet of commercial yogurt, did not develop cataracts; even the baby rats, who had not yet developed the enzyme necessary to digest the galactose, were normal and cataract free.

It's probably wise, however, to stay away from yogurt if you have galactokinase deficiency, until, at least, more extensive research is conducted.

Yogurt is Alive!

One of the virtues of yogurt is that it is a "live" food. The bacteria in yogurt are very much alive when you eat it, and remain alive on their way through your system to do their healthful handiwork in your large intestine.

One researcher has gone so far as to theorize that yogurt is so alive, that like plants, it has emotions and can feel pain and pleasure. Cleve Backster, author of *The Secret Life Of Plants,* did an experiment with yogurts and electrodes. He put two electrodes in one container of yogurt, and poured a little milk into a second container, sitting nearby. Almost immediately, Backster reported, the electrodes in the first container registered some electrical activity. Backster claimed this was a response, that the yogurt with the electrodes was showing an emotional reaction to the milk added to the other container of yogurt. He wasn't certain whether the yogurt was pleased or jealous, only that it was definitely moved.

Perhaps Backster's experiments might explain why some people have said that yogurt is a kind of emotional barometer. On New York City's Madison Avenue, lunch-counter owners, who cater to the frenzied advertising crowd, say that if a product, a show, or an ad campaign is not faring well, the majority of their ad-agency customers order yogurt. But in California, eating yogurt is a sign of another emotional predicament. People out there say eating lots of yogurt is a sign of being in love.

Until much more extensive and thorough research is done on yogurt, the controversy over its healthful benefits will rage on. Yogurt is still so much a fledgling food in the United States, despite its mushrooming popularity, that there are no national yogurt-manufacturers associations or standards of identity for the product. As far as the other foods we consume and buy at the grocery store, yogurt is still the new kid on the shelf.

Yogurt, at least for a large majority of people, is a very good thing. It may not be the Fountain of Youth that everyone is searching for, but it will make the years more enjoyable because it makes for better health. It may not be the magic all-purpose healer, but there are many ailments that yogurt can either cure or alleviate. It probably won't make you look like Cybill Shepherd or Robert Redford, but eating yogurt will undoubtedly make you feel better, and that's a large part of the battle to looking good.

[4]

OUTER YOGURT

The early Persians were not content merely to use their beloved yogurt at mealtimes—they had other uses for the fermented milk product stored in their earthenware pots. The Persian women, as anxious as today's women about facial lines and creases and other signs of aging, applied yogurt to their faces to smooth away wrinkles and erase impurities. Dabbing yogurt on their faces like a vanishing cream, these clever Persian females realized the outer values of yogurt as well as its inner values. It only stood to reason, they figured, that something that could work such wonders *in* your body could work similar wonders *on* your body.

The beauty-conscious women of antiquity did not have the array of commercial products available today. They had to make their own cosmetics, using their ingenuity and the plants and fruits in their environments. They continually experimented with all kinds of foods and natural substances to determine what would be good for what—which herb would help tighten the pores and which fruit would restore moisture to their skins. More often than not, yogurt was an essential ingredient in their homemade beauty remedies.

After all, they knew that eating yogurt was a step toward beauty. When yogurt was eaten on a daily basis, they found that the sour milk culture contributed to clearer and smoother skin; more lustrous, healthier hair; shining eyes; and stronger nails. And when they applied yogurt as a facial, these women discovered that their wrinkles disappeared and their complexions looked more youthful and more translucent. Yogurt may not have been the magic answer for transforming an ugly duckling into a raving beauty, but the Persian women relied on it for good looks, much as a contemporary woman uses her expensive store-bought creams and lotions.

What's in yogurt that makes it an effective cosmetic? The high protein and calcium content contributes to its beneficial effects when rubbed on the skin. Just as the proteins, minerals, and vitamins nourish your body, so do they nourish your skin. The lactic acid in yogurt makes it especially good as a bleaching agent for freckles and other discolorations. The B vitamins also add to its effectiveness as a beauty aid for skin.

People with oily or dull and lifeless skin find that yogurt used as a facial perks up their complexions, gives them a rosy glow, and can even help to clear up blemishes. Other women with blotchy, unevenly colored complexions have discovered that yogurt facials applied regularly make for more uniform skin coloration. And women plagued with bumps and knobs and other skin imperfections say that yogurt massaged into their pores every night gives their skin a finer, more even, satiny texture.

Just as yogurt can be the versatile ingredient in almost any kind of food recipe, and can be included in soups and appetizers as well as desserts and beverages, so too can yogurt be used cosmetically in many different ways. Facials, masks, conditioners, rinses, lotions, salves—you name it—can all be made by mixing yogurt with a variety of natural ingredients, like herbs, fruits, honey, or eggs.

But the simplest, and yet an also extremely effective, yogurt cosmetic is just virgin yogurt. Yogurt alone, with nothing else added, is dabbed thickly on the face and allowed to remain, either for a few hours or overnight. Then, in the morning, the dried yogurt is rinsed away. This preparation can be as beautifying as some high-priced chemical concoctions from a department-store cosmetic counter.

Many companies who specialize in natural beauty products use yogurt in their recipes. The International Yogurt Company in Los Angeles markets both a yogurt face powder and a yogurt face cream. Another natural-beauty-product company offered a strawberry yogurt shampoo to the public for a while. The shampoo was great on the hair, but its appearance in the bottle left much to be desired. The yogurt apparently separated from the rest of the ingredients, which was not especially aesthetically pleasing. The shampoo simply did not look pretty, so the product had to be taken off the market.

Of course, if you're a true yogurt pioneer, you'll pass up the ready-made yogurt cosmetics in favor of whipping up your own beauty potions. Soon you'll be shunning the gooey gels and pore-clogging blushers on the cosmetic counters and turning to those preparations made from the finest ingredients available, life-giving nutritious food found in your own kitchen. With the addition of some everyday foods from your refrigerator, you can make any number of yogurt cosmetics. They're certainly cheaper than the remedies found at the drugstore, free of harmful chemicals, and undoubtedly much more fun. Just be sure that you have enough yogurt left over to eat!

A Few Words of Advice About Homemade Cosmetics

If you have especially sensitive skin or are prone to allergic reactions, you should make a patch test on a small area of your skin before you try a recipe. Also, if the slightest bit of irritation or redness develops after using a certain recipe, then that preparation is not for you. Your skin condition can change through the years, and a mask that once was perfectly suited to your oily skin may later cause flaking and scaling as your skin loses its quantity of oil with the passing of time. So use your homemade potions with care.

Since yogurt is a "live" food and does not last forever, you should make only as much of a cosmetic as you need for one or two applications. The freshest yogurt makes the best cosmetics. Just as yogurt's nutritional values diminish as it ages, so its beautifying properties lessen. Be sure to refrigerate your cosmetics as soon as possible and use the leftovers in a few days. Once you get the hang of pampering yourself with homemade yogurt cosmetics, you'll want to try new recipes all the time. You won't want to stick with just one kind of mask or facial, but will want to experiment as much as possible.

Before using any of the facials or masks made from yogurt, make sure your face is clean and free of makeup. Take care also that you avoid the ultrasensitive area around and under the eyes.

A good guide for checking whether a yogurt cosmetic is beneficial for your skin or hair type is to analyze the ingredients included in the recipe. If an acidic fruit like lemon is used, the cosmetic will have an astringent quality and will probably be more helpful to oily skins. A rich, oil-laden fruit like avocado or banana will be better for dry skins. In addition, many fruits and vegetables, like the papaya, have particular enzymes which have specific effects.

Natural Ingredients

Following are a variety of beauty recipes which all rely on yogurt. You can start with these and then blend your own inspirations, choosing from any of the fruits, vegetables, and herbs below, depending on your individual needs.

ASTRINGENTS

· *Fruits and vegetables*—carrot, pear, strawberry, cucumber, honeydew, tomato, apple, parsley, potato, lemon, orange.

· *Herbs*—elder, fennel, lemongrass, sage, rosemary, nettle, comfrey root, yarrow, peppermint, cornflower, clover blossom.

OILS

· *Fruits and vegetables*—apricot, avocado, banana, fig, artichoke, coconut, raisins.

· *Herbs*—camomile, rose hips, orange blossom.

For the Face

Masks can be applied once or twice a week for good results—but use more often or less frequently is O.K. too.

HONEY-YOGURT MASK

Mix about two teaspoons honey with about four teaspoons yogurt. Beat the mixture well. Apply to face. This is effective in banishing wrinkles.

YOGURT AND BREWER'S YEAST MASK

Combine enough yogurt with a few teaspoons brewer's yeast to make a thick paste. The mixture should be fluid enough so that it can be spread easily on the face. Apply to neck and face area, and allow to remain until the mixture is completely dry. Rinse off after 20 to 30 minutes, using a facecloth dipped in warm water. Rub gently. If the area under the eye seems very dry, apply a little oil here.

The yeast in the mask contracts and draws the blood to the skin to feed and cleanse it. The blood movement increases and the effect is very stimulating to the complexion. The yogurt in the mask enhances and adds to the B vitamins in the yeast. The mask produces a rosy glow, with a vibrant, ageless look.

YOGURT-TOMATO PICKUP

Combine two tablespoons yogurt with one-quarter cup tomato juice. If you can use a fresh tomato for the juice (strained), so much the better. Whip up the ingredients in a blender until well mixed. Apply to face with cotton and allow to remain for about 15 minutes. Rinse off, using warm water—never hot!

YOGURT-EGG MOISTURIZER

Combine one tablespoon yogurt with one egg yolk. Make sure the yolk is well beaten into the yogurt. Spread on face thoroughly, using cotton or a soft brush. After 30 minutes, rinse off with warm water.

YOGURT-HONEY MOISTURIZER

Mix equal parts of honey and yogurt, several tablespoons each. Add enough flour to make a paste, which should not be too thick. Dab on face. Remove after 10 to 15 minutes with a damp facecloth.

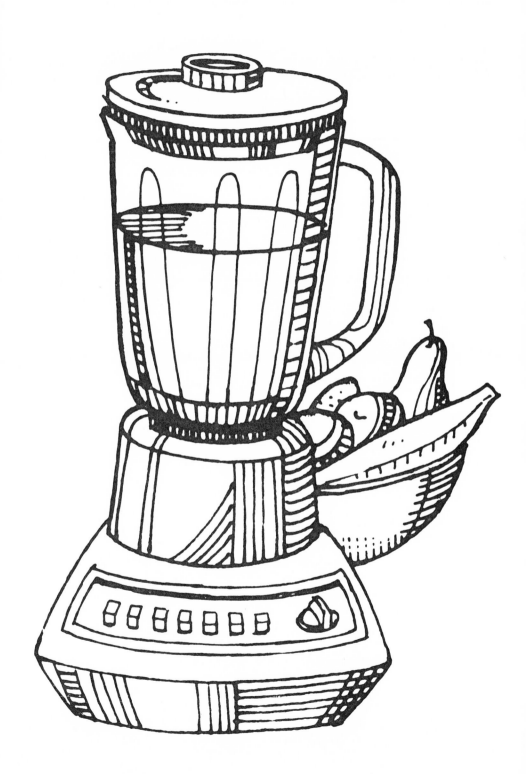

PEACHY-KEEN YOGURT MASK

Peel a small peach and puree it until liquified in a blender. Add several teaspoons yogurt. Pat on face, using cotton pads. Rinse off after 20 minutes with lukewarm water.

APPLE MASK

Peel a medium-size apple. Puree the apple in a blender, after first removing the seeds and core. Add several teaspoons yogurt and blend well. Apply to face. Allow to remain for 30 minutes. Rinse off with warm water. If your skin is especially oily, follow up with a splash of cool water.

HERBAL YOGURT MASK

Steep several teaspoons rosemary or dried mint leaves in a small amount of hot water. When the mixture has cooled, add a few teaspoons yogurt. Make sure the mixture has cooled; otherwise the yogurt will curdle. Blend well and smooth on face. Leave on for about 20 to 30 minutes. Rinse off with warm water.

YOGURT AND PAPAYA FRESHENER

Peel a papaya and puree the fruit in a blender. Mix the pureed fruit with a few teaspoons yogurt. Apply the combination to face and allow it to remain for 15 to 20 minutes. Rinse off.

This freshener is especially good for skin that has a sallow, wan look, like after late hours and little sleep. The papaya has an enzyme in it called papain which absorbs dead tissue and helps slough off those lifeless bits of skin.

YOGURT-CAMOMILE MOISTURIZER

Prepare about one-eighth cup strong camomile tea. Mix with equal parts of honey and yogurt. Apply to face—if mixture is very fluid, use cotton pads or a soft brush. Rinse off after 20 to 30 minutes, using a soft washcloth.

This facial is especially good for dry and chapped skin, particularly in those cold winter months. The camomile tea soothes the skin, and the honey, combined with the yogurt, leaves a beneficial film on the face that prevents moisture from evaporating. Thus the skin rejuvenates itself and doesn't lose that valuable water content.

LEMON-YOGURT TONER

Squeeze the juice of half a fresh lemon. Strain. Combine with about three tablespoons yogurt. Smooth on skin and allow to remain for 15 to 30 minutes. This mask is especially good for oily skin, because the acid in the lemon juice cuts the grease and grime. Furthermore, the yogurt helps to improve the uneven texture that is often characteristic of troubled or oily skin.

ALMOND-YOGURT CLEANSER

Blend a few tablespoons almond meal with enough yogurt to make a paste that is easy to apply. Almond meal can be prepared at home in a blender—simply use some blanched, skinless almonds and grate until very finely cut. Almond meal can also be purchased from various cosmetic supplies stores that carry natural products.

With your fingertips, massage face gently with this paste, using a circular motion. Allow to dry. Remove with a rinse of warm water, following up with splashes of cool water—not icy cold—to close the pores. This mask is effective for helping remove blackheads and toning up enlarged pores. If skin is severely broken out, however, this mask should not be used, since the abrasive quality will only further inflame pimples and pustules.

AVOCADO-YOGURT CONDITIONER

Peel half an avocado and puree the fruit in a blender. Combine with an equal amount of yogurt. Apply to face and leave on for about 30 minutes or, if desired, overnight. Rinse off with warm water. The oil in the avocado will serve as an emollient to restore moisture and oil to dry, undernourished skin victimized by bad weather.

YOGURT FRECKLE BLEACH

Simply apply yogurt to blotchy or discolored areas of the skin, wherever you want a more uniform skin tone. When the yogurt is dry, rinse off with cool water. Regular use should help to achieve even skin coloration. If the skin feels dry after the yogurt bleach, dab on a few teaspoons oil to prevent irritation.

OATMEAL-YOGURT FACE WASH

Mix equal parts of oatmeal and yogurt, to form a thin paste. Apply to face and allow to dry. Remove after 15 to 20 minutes, with a warm washcloth. The oatmeal combined with yogurt has a soothing and softening effect on the skin and is particularly good for irritated complexions. The oatmeal also cuts the oil in troubled skin and can serve to lessen the red and irritated look of blemishes. This mask is especially good for people with sensitive and troubled skin, since many abrasive masks are irritating.

BANANA-YOGURT FACIAL

Mash one small banana thoroughly. Mix with yogurt. Smear the mixture on face, using cotton or a shaving brush if necessary. Rinse off with warm water after 30 minutes. The banana is rich in oil, which creates a protective film on the face, thereby cutting down on loss of moisture. Good for dry skin.

ELDER-YOGURT ASTRINGENT

Pour about one cup boiling water over one tablespoon elder. Allow to steep for about 30 minutes. Strain and discard herbs. When the mixture is cool, combine with about one cup yogurt. Apply to skin and allow to dry. Rinse off with cool water. The elder mixed with the yogurt has an astringent effect and is beneficial to oily skin.

YOGURT AND FULLER'S EARTH MASK

Combine about one rounded teaspoon fuller's earth (available in most drugstores) with enough yogurt to make a paste. Smear on face and allow to remain for 10 to 15 minutes. The mask will dry and harden, and you won't be able to talk. Rinse off with warm water.

Like brewer's yeast and yogurt mask, this also has tightening qualities that increase the blood movement and revitalize the complexion. After the mask is removed, you will notice that your skin seems recharged with color. Good for normal and oily skins.

STRAWBERRY-YOGURT REJUVENATOR

Mash a handful of strawberries to a pulp. Add one egg and a few teaspoons yogurt. Apply to face and leave on for about 20 minutes.

This mask will tone up your pores, enrich your skin, and help to erase lines and wrinkles.

FENNEL WRINKLE REMOVER

Make about one cup strong fennel tea. Combine one teaspoon of it with equal parts of honey and yogurt, a few teaspoons each. Apply to face and allow to remain for 20 minutes. Rinse off with tepid water.

ELDER FLOWER-YOGURT TONIC

Mix a small amount of dried elder flowers with a few teaspoons yogurt. Apply with cotton. After 15 minutes, rinse with warm water.

The elder combines with the yogurt to act as an astringent, toning up the pores and cleansing and purifying the skin.

PEAR-YOGURT FACIAL

Mash one small ripe pear, removing the stem and seeds. Mix with about one-quarter cup yogurt. Blend well and dab on face. Leave on for about 20 to 30 minutes. Rinse off thoroughly, using a washcloth.

The pear has an astringent quality and will help to ease off dead skin, thus making for a glowing complexion.

BARLEY-YOGURT TONER

Simmer one teaspoon barley in one cup water for several minutes, until the barley is tender. Cool the mixture. Combine with one-half cup yogurt and apply to face and neck area. Allow to remain for 30 minutes, and then remove with warm water.

The barley will tone up and rejuvenate tired skin.

VINEGAR-YOGURT ASTRINGENT

Mix about two teaspoons apple-cider vinegar with several teaspoons yogurt. Apply to face. Leave on for about 20 to 30 minutes. Remove with warm water, following up with splashes of cold water to tighten the pores.

The mask is very good for troubled skin subject to blemishes. The vinegar and yogurt combination clears and refines the skin, preventing more serious conditions.

For the Bath

YOGURT-HERB BATH

Steep one tablespoon of your favorite dried herb, such as thyme, mint, rosemary, sage, or basil, in one cup boiling water. Allow to remain overnight. Strain the liquid and combine with one cup yogurt. Mix in a few teaspoons oil, such as wheat-germ oil, olive oil, or any good cold-pressed oil from a health-food store. Use about one-half to one cup in your bathwater. You can also add a few drops of your favorite cologne if you wish. The leftover mixture should be stored in the refrigerator.

ZESTY YOGURT BATH

Good for those evenings when you're dog tired but must go out. Mix a few tablespoons baking soda with a few tablespoons cornstarch. Mix with about one-half cup yogurt and add immediately to your running bathwater. The baking soda will add a tingling feeling to your bath and refresh your weary body. (You can substitute Epsom salts for the baking soda for the same kind of pick-me-up.)

HERBAL GELATIN BATH

Prepare one-half cup of your favorite herbal tea, at full strength. Mix this with one teaspoon unflavored gelatin, such as Knox, and about one-half cup yogurt. Blend well. When you're ready for your bath, scoop up a few tablespoons and hold it under running water.

The gelatin and the yogurt create a protein-filled bath, which is a terrific rejuvenator for a fatigued body. This mixture has very good cleansing qualities.

YOGURT-OIL BATH

In a blender, combine one cup oil with one cup yogurt. Mix well. For each bath, add a few tablespoons to the water and swish well to make sure the mixture is well combined.

This is especially beneficial to dry and chapped skin in the winter.

For the Hair

AVOCADO-YOGURT HAIR CONDITIONER

Peel one avocado and either mash the fruit or puree in a blender. For best results, the avocado should be very ripe. Blend this with about one-half cup yogurt, adding enough to make a creamy mixture. Massage the avocado and yogurt combination well into your hair and scalp. Allow to remain for 45 to 60 minutes. Rinse out and then follow up with your regular shampoo. This hair treatment helps to restore the oils in dry hair and increases the shine.

YOGURT-OIL HAIR TREATMENT

Mix one cup yogurt with two to three tablespoons oil, such as sesame, safflower, soy, etc. Massage into hair and scalp, spreading onto the ends of the hair, which may be dried and split. Allow to remain for about 45 minutes. Rinse out and then shampoo.

EGG-YOGURT CONDITIONER

Mix one egg yolk with one cup yogurt. Make sure the yolk is well beaten into the yogurt. Apply to towel-dried, freshly shampooed hair. Leave on for about 20 to 30 minutes, after combing thoroughly through the hair. Rinse well, using warm water first and then following up with cool water.

YOGURT SETTING LOTION

Dilute one-half cup yogurt with one-half cup water. Use while setting hair to add body and to hold the set. If hair is very fine and does not retain curl and wave very well, use full-strength yogurt. However, this may get very sticky!

HERBAL YOGURT SHAMPOO

Combine one teaspoon yogurt with several teaspoons herbal shampoo. Blend well. Apply to hair as usual, and rinse out thoroughly.

The casein in the yogurt provides a thin coating of protection to the hair, which guards against pollution and drying winds.

For the Body

YOGURT AFTER-SUN CONDITIONER

Apply yogurt to parts of face and body that have been exposed to the sun. Allow to remain for 45 to 60 minutes. Remove in warm shower.

YOGURT-ALTHEA SUNBURN TREATMENT

Steep one or two tablespoons althea leaves in one cup boiling water. When this mixture is cool, strain. Mix with one cup yogurt, at room temperature. Apply to afflicted areas, and leave on for about 60 minutes. Rinse off gently in a lukewarm shower.

ALMOND MEAL-YOGURT ABRASIVE

Combine almond meal with enough yogurt to make a thick paste. Using a circular motion, rub on any rough or calloused areas on body where dead skin has accumulated, such as heels, bottom of feet, elbows, hands, or knees. Rub the paste, allow to remain for 30 minutes. Remove with a washcloth dipped in warm water.

Once you start getting into yogurt cosmetics, you'll undoubtedly begin making two batches of yogurt at once—one for meals and one for beauty!

[5]

HOW TO MAKE YOGURT

Did you know that 10 percent of all yogurt eaters make their own? Perhaps that's not enough to make the commercial producers worry about sales, but it's a steadily growing figure for a variety of reasons.

Why Do It Yourself?

First of all, it's pretty easy to do. All you need is a quart of milk that's been heated to the boiling point (212°F.) and allowed to cool down to 115°F.; a tablespoon of "starter"—yogurt from a container, a friend, or any other source; something to put it in; and a place or a way to keep it at the same, constant temperature while it incubates for several hours. Once you have the mechanics down pat, your active participation is less than an hour.

Secondly, making your own yogurt is part of the whole "going natural" movement that's been a permanent fixture in the last decade. If you can grow your own vegetables or sew your own clothes, you can certainly make your own yogurt. (It's not absolutely necessary, like author Ken Kesey, to raise your own cows so you can have total control over everything from feed to milk, but it's not all that unusual, either.)

Thirdly, maybe even most importantly, making your own yogurt is cheaper than buying it. A quart of homemade costs less than half of what the same amount costs in the store—and that includes the electricity to run a yogurt maker or some other electric heating source. For an 8-ounce cup of store-bought yogurt, the price can be as high as 45¢. The cost of eight 8-ounce servings made at home—including the price of a half gallon of milk (about 80¢) and electricity—runs about 10¢ a serving, a saving of over 75 percent.

Another good reason for making your own yogurt is to maintain tighter calorie control. If you add your own fresh fruit, preserves, flavorings, etc., just before you're ready to eat, you can limit the quantity according to your taste or diet. As we've said before, fruit preserves (like those in commercial yogurts) only add calories.

You will also have full control over quality and taste, something that's particularly important to a concerned consumer. There's no need to add chemical preservatives to lengthen shelf life, artificial flavors and colors to make it more attractive, sugar or whatever to enhance the taste.

By carefully choosing your starter, you can control even the strains of bacteria that go into your yogurt, and include some (for example, *Lactobacillus acidophilus,* which is thought to have a particularly beneficial effect on the digestive system) not usually found in commercial brands.

Probably the best reason of all for making your own yogurt is that it's the freshest way to get it. You know it hasn't been sitting on a shelf for several days before you take it home, and of course, the fresher yogurt is, the sweeter it is, because it hasn't had time to acidify and turn sour. What you should get with your homemade brew is a rich, creamy, custardy, just slightly tart yogurt.

What Will You Need?

MILK

Almost any kind will do—cow's, goat's, sheep's, raw, skim, evaporated, even soybean milk—it's all a matter of taste and availability. As long as the milk is fresh (the older it is, the longer it takes to incubate, and the more starter you need), and neither presweetened (except in certain circumstances, see page 69) nor thickened with anything like cornstarch, tapioca, or chemical emulsifiers (which will interfere with the culturing process), it's still milk. For a quart of yogurt, you'll need a quart of milk; the taste and consistency will vary with the kind you choose.

Whole milk. This will result in a dense, creamy yogurt, slightly tart, with all the vitamins and nutrients of milk, plus the little extras that the yogurting process adds. Eight ounces of whole-milk yogurt has 160 calories (the same as a glass of milk). Use as is, right out of the container or bottle, or add 2 tablespoons powdered milk for extra thickness.

Skim milk. With skim milk, you'll get the same type of thick, custardy, sweet-tasting yogurt as with whole; the same protein and mineral values (except for slightly less of the vitamins A, D, E, K, because they are fat soluble and the fat is removed from skim milk); and fewer calories (120) to boot. You must add ⅓ cup additional nonfat dry milk powder per quart of skim milk to bring it up to the same consistency of whole milk.

Evaporated milk. This is whole milk that has had half the moisture removed and then has been canned. It must be reconstituted with water. It's a bit more fattening than whole milk, 173 calories per 8 ounces, but the yogurt made from it will be thick and creamy, and, needless to say, delicious.

To make a large batch of yogurt with evaporated milk, combine one 13-ounce can with 5 cups hot water and 3 cups nonfat dry milk powder. You'll need to add ½ cup starter at the "add starter" point, and after about 6 to 8 hours, you'll have 2 quarts of yogurt.

Condensed milk. This is actually evaporated milk (with 60 percent of the water removed) to which sugar has been added. A 14½-ounce can is equal nutritionally to 2½ cups milk plus ½ cup (8 tablespoons) sugar. Yogurt made with condensed milk will naturally be sweeter and more caloric than others (about 275 calories per 8 ounces, plain), and the traditional tartness will be masked by the sugar.

For a sweetened yogurt, combine 2½ cups water, 1 cup nonfat dry milk powder, ⅔ cup sweetened condensed milk and 3 tablespoons yogurt.

Soybean milk. Similar in taste, texture, and consistency to whole milk, soybean milk is different nutritionally, basically lacking in iodine and other nutrients. Yogurt from soybean milk will be tasty, creamy, with a slightly nutty flavor. Calorically, 8 ounces of soybean milk has 80 calories. You'll need ¼ cup regular starter per quart of soy milk—because the nutritive properties are different from regular milk and therefore react differently to the yogurt culture. If you're starting with yogurt already made from soy milk, you'll need 1 cup starter for each new batch of yogurt.

To make soybean milk, first wash and soak soybeans overnight in enough water to cover. Drain and rinse, and put 1 cup beans plus 3 cups fresh water in a blender; blend till pulpy (or put through a food grinder, pouring water over them as you grind). Use up all the beans this way. Put the pulp in a stainless steel, glass, or porcelain pan (not aluminum) and simmer for about 15 minutes. Then strain through a sieve or double thickness of cheesecloth.

An easier method might be to buy soybean flour in a health-food store and mix 1 quart of it with 4 cups water. Then strain through a cloth bag, and simmer the resulting liquid in the top of a double boiler for 15 minutes. With either method, soybean milk can be easily substituted for regular milk in cooking and drinking, as well as yogurt making. Perhaps its greatest benefit comes from its milklike taste, without the allergic reaction sometimes caused by cow's milk.

Other types of milk. True yogurt aficionados claim that raw morning milk is the best kind to use for yogurt, but it must be pasteurized first to kill any bacteria that not only might interfere with the yogurt bacilli, but also may be harmful to you. Raw milk is available in health-food stores, usually by a doctor's prescription only.

Goat's milk will give you a yogurt that's superthick, high in butterfat (although, only 163 calories per 8 ounces), and very rich—too rich for many people who find it hard to digest.

Water buffalo's milk is also rich, with a consequently rich yogurt, and ass's milk will give you yogurt that's easily digestible, with a fine curd and sweet taste.

Once you've chosen the type of milk to use, the next step is selecting the starter.

STARTER

What turns milk into yogurt is the action of a living population of bacteria—most often, *Lactobacillus Bulgaricus* and *Streptococcus thermophilus*—on warm milk. It can be perpetuated, almost indefinitely, by introducing an already existent culture into fresh milk, passing on, in that way, the qualities and bacterial strains of the original. In some places, the original culture is many years old. Yonah Schimmel's, a New York landmark restaurant, has a yogurt that has been perpetuated for over fifty years, starting when the original Yonah arrived in New York from Eastern Europe, with a little package of the family's yogurt tucked in his baggage. It's been passed down for generations, and the yogurt available at Yonah Schimmel's today is a direct descendant, in taste and purity, of the original.

It's not necessary to use starter that's fifty years old. Any good one will do—*good* meaning you like the taste and the qualities of the yogurt it comes from. And the starter can be had in two forms.

One tablespoon of yogurt. You can get this from a friend, from commercial types available in supermarkets or health-food stores, or from your local neighborhood Middle Eastern restaurant (which most probably makes its own).

It should be fresh, unflavored yogurt, and not pasteurized after the culture has been added. The fresher the starter is, the sweeter your yogurt, and the less time it will take to incubate. Flavored yogurt will work, but you'll be stuck with a quart of yogurt with a specific taste, good for eating only as is.

Which starter you choose will determine what your yogurt tastes like, depending of course, on the type of milk you use. A highly acidic culture will obviously result in a yogurt with an acidy content; a sweeter starter will give you a sweeter end product.

The bacterial strains are also affected by your choice of starter. With commercial yogurt, you will be perpetuating the two common yogurt bacteria, *bulgaricus* and *thermophilus*. But if, for example, you begin with acidophilus yogurt, you will be adding a strain of *Lactobacillus acidophilus* to your homemade yogurt.

Dried culture. Ultimately, you will still have yogurt, but starting with a dried culture has both its advantages and disadvantages. By buying a dried culture, you can find a wider variety of strains. For example, Bulgarian yogurt cultures are imported in powdered form, as are those from France and other European countries. But dried cultures are much harder to find. Health-food stores are one source, although the cultures are not always stocked in great quantity because they are not often called for. Mail order is about the only other way to get dried cultures, and a listing of sources is available on page 121. You can store dried culture much longer than fresh yogurt, without being concerned about losing freshness. On the other hand, the incubation period is much longer—sometimes as much as 24 hours—than with an active starter. Dried yogurt culture is expensive, about $2.50 for a packet that will make a quart. In any case, it's fun to experiment, and once you've got your own yogurt going, your only expense is milk.

Now you're ready to begin the actual process of making yogurt.

Method
HEATING THE MILK

Whatever type of milk you've chosen, it should be brought just to the boil in order to kill all the existing bacteria in the milk itself, so they don't overwhelm the bacteria in the starter.

Use a stainless steel, glass, or enamel pot—never lead or aluminum, which can leave harmful residues in the milk. To avoid overboiling or scorching, a double boiler is the best solution (the slightly burned taste of overboiled milk is unpleasant, and will carry into the yogurt). If a skin should form while the milk is heating, remove it with a wooden spoon. If it's not removed, it won't mix back into the milk, and will throw off the entire operation.

COOLING

For the starter culture to remain alive, the milk must be cooled down before it is introduced. The bacteria will live and multiply quite happily at anywhere from 90°F. to 120°F., but 115°F. seems to be the optimal temperature for growth.

You can test the temperature in any number of ways. The most scientific, of course, is with a simple kitchen or darkroom thermometer. If none is available, try dipping your elbow (a clean one) into the milk, like testing a baby's bath. If the milk feels neither too hot nor too cold, just slightly above body temperature, it's ready. Or sprinkle a little milk on your wrist; it should feel the same as when you test a baby's bottle. Or simply dip a clean finger into the milk; if it's cool

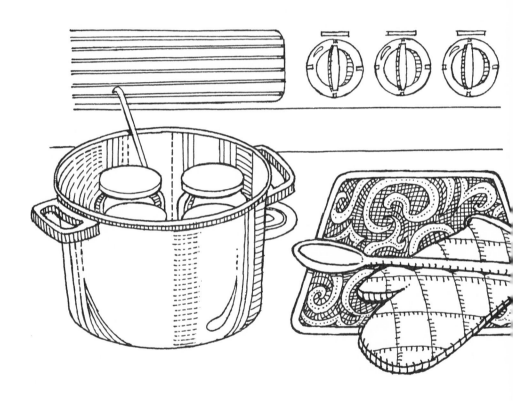

enough to hold your finger there while you count to twenty, you're ready to go on.

The cooling step takes about half an hour at normal room temperature. Make sure that your thermometer, elbow, finger, or whatever you're using to test with is scrupulously clean, so you don't reintroduce any unwanted bacteria into the milk.

ADDING THE STARTER

Into the milk, cooled to 115°F., add one heaping tablespoon of starter per quart. In this case, more is not better. Too much starter, and the bacilli will be crowded into making a lumpy yogurt; too little and it just won't yog. Remember that for yogurt made with soybean, evaporated, or condensed milk, you need more starter; for anything else, one heaping tablespoon is plenty. Mix the starter well into the milk; whether you're using dried or regular, it should be evenly distributed. Don't beat or whip the mixture, or you'll break down the components so that they won't gel.

INCUBATION

There are many schools of thought about this next step, going back as far as the nomads in the desert who let it all hang out in a skin bag. However you go about it, the purpose is to maintain the mixture at the optimum temperature for life and growth. Below 90°F., the yogurt bacteria will be alive, but inactive. Above 120°F., they will be dead. 115°F. is best.

With an electric yogurt maker. This is the easiest way to maintain a constant temperature during the incubation period. There are a number of yogurt makers on the market, all inexpensive to run because they maintain a low heat level—in fact, they are probably the cheapest, electrically, of all kitchen appliances to use, for just that reason. They are also inexpensive to buy, ranging in price from $9 to $15.

The electric yogurt makers are all similar in operation. There is some kind of electric heating element to provide a constant temperature; ceramic or glass jars to hold the yogurt; explicit directions; recipes; even a packet of starter in some cases. Only one, the Salton yogurt maker (which is also probably the most widely available), claims to be thermostatically controlled, but whether or not this is vital has not been determined. If you follow the instructions, they do take the guesswork out of keeping the temperature constant, but non-machine methods, though a little less exact, have worked for thousands of years.

There's no reason, if you choose one of those, why it shouldn't work for you.

Without a yogurt maker. The first thing you have to do is pour the well-stirred milk and starter mixture into something. Crockery, earthenware, stoneware, and glass containers are best; metal may be eroded by the acidity. Peanut-butter, mayonnaise, or almost any other wide-mouth jars work fine; ceramic custard cups, covered casseroles, mixing bowls, or whatever you have available will do, too. Covers can either be whatever comes with the utensil; or fashioned from brown paper, aluminum foil, kitchen parchment, etc., and fastened with a rubber band.

Once your yogurt is poured and covered, you can choose from any one of the following incubation methods, or come up with your own. To make certain that the one you select works for you, you must test it out thoroughly, using plain water, to be sure you can keep a temperature constant for 10 to 20 hours. If your method will keep water at 115°F. for that amount of time, it will keep yogurt, too. Don't expect to succeed without some experimentation. Trial and error is the basis of any successful venture, and yogurt making is no exception to the rule.

Electric heat sources. A general rule of thumb for all these incubation methods is to make sure the water your container sits in is 115°F. to begin with, and that the water level in the outer container meets the yogurt level in the inner one.

1. An electric skillet, big enough to hold a covered container or several jars of the yogurt mixture, filled with hot water and turned to the previously determined correct temperature setting to hold it at 115°F. Make sure the skillet is deep enough so the water comes up to the same level as the yogurt in the container.

2. An electric hot tray or food warmer, probably set somewhere between medium and low. Put your container or jars of yogurt into a large pot (cast iron is a particularly good conductor of heat); fill with hot water to the same level as the yogurt, and set on the tray. You've tested, of course, to see at precisely what setting the tray will maintain water in a cast-iron pot at 115°F.

3. An electric heating pad or blanket, set at the temperature that will allow a skillet filled with hot water, and your container of yogurt, to sit on it, and keep at 115°F.

The layaway plan. There are a number of ordinary household things that radiate enough heat to maintain yogurt at 115°F. for the number of hours necessary, without your having to do anything special.

As an extra insulator, where applicable, immerse your covered container or jars in a large pot of hot water first; then follow our directions.

1. Your oven. If it's a gas oven with a pilot light, that can provide sufficient heat, especially if you put a pan of hot water on the rack directly below the yogurt, and keep the door closed. If it's not warm enough, or there is no pilot light, turn the oven up to 120°F.; then let it cool down to 115°F. with the door ajar (about two minutes). If it gets too cool, turn it on again, briefly, with the door open, until you've found the right temperature; then close the door.

In an electric oven, turn the setting to the lowest, (usually "warm"), and put the yogurt on the middle rack. If it's too hot, move the rack up a notch or two, and keep the oven door open a crack.

2. On top of the stove. If there's a pilot light, set the yogurt directly over it; if it's too hot, raise the container with a rack (the metal kind you cool cakes on will do fine). Use the same method with an electric stove, setting the container of yogurt on any element set at the lowest heat.

3. A wide-mouth thermos jar will hold yogurt at the same temperature at which it is put in. Rinse the thermos in hot water first to get the inside warmed up. No water bath is necessary here. A thermos is a natural insulator. Chill the yogurt in the thermos for several hours after the incubation period is over, and then remove it from the jar.

4. Wrap a warm quilt or comforter, a heavy blanket, thick towels, etc., around your covered container of yogurt, and set it in or near any constantly warm place: radiator; hot-air floor register; heating ducts; banked woodstove fire; the warm area behind the refrigerator (not on top, because the vibrations of the motor will disturb the milk and keep it from yogging). This is a traditional, tried and true method that has been used successfully for hundreds of years.

5. Set the covered container or jars of yogurt in a wooden cabinet that has an electric light bulb (about 15 watts) inside it. Be sure to check the temperature carefully; a smaller bulb may be sufficient, or a larger one necessary. A similar method is to line a heavy carton with felt, put your yogurt inside, and suspend a light bulb over it.

6. Hot-water bottles, filled with water at 115°F., can be placed under or wrapped around your container of yogurt.

7. Make a yogurt incubator, sometimes called a "hay box" or a "fireless cooker." This is simply a small wooden or heavy cardboard box, large enough to hold your container or jars of yogurt, placed inside a slightly larger one. The space between the two is insulated with hay, vermiculite chips, sawdust, wood shavings, feathers, straw, rags, newspapers, etc. Both boxes are covered and set to rest in a warm place.

8. Polystyrene ice bucket or food chest: Pour hot water into the bottom, enough to reach the same level as the yogurt in the container, and cover tightly.

We can't stress enough the need for keeping the temperature a constant 115°F. during incubation. This might mean a lot of testing with water beforehand—if you disturb the yogurt too often while it's incubating, you'll wind up close, but no cigar. The perfect temperature is 115°F. A temperature of 114°F. or 116°F. will not be fatal, but the more even the temperature remains, the faster the yogurt will culture.

IS IT YOGURT YET?

Timing is a delicate part of your yogurt making. It can take as little as 3 to 4 hours in a thermos jar; as much as 15 to 20 hours (no matter which incubating method you use) the first time you make yogurt with a dried starter. You will have to experiment by checking every few hours. But not too often—ten minutes means nothing in the life of a batch of yogurt. Check the first time after about 6 hours, then perhaps, 3 or 4 hours later. Gently tip the container to the side to see if it's thickened. If it's not, put it away and come back later. A lot of things can affect the timing: in the summer, it always seems to take a little longer; humidity, drafts, vibrations, all seem to play a part in how long it takes, as does the age of the milk and the starter.

Whatever you do, don't overincubate. If the yogurt is thickened at all, put it in the refrigerator. It will go on thickening for a time while it's cooling. Overincubation will give you yogurt that's tough, tarter, higher in lactic acid, and lower in living and beneficial bacteria. Refrigeration will firm the body and prevent the yogurt from becoming too sour. Let it sit in the refrigerator for 12 to 24 hours before eating to let it set and chill properly.

After 24 hours in the refrigerator, your yogurt should be nice and firm and ready to eat. If there's a watery separation on the top, it's only whey. Don't stir it in, spill it off. It won't mix back into the yogurt well, and you won't be losing anything by getting rid of it. Save it, if you like, to use in place of other liquids in cooking.

Yogurt tastes best when it's fresh—sweeter and creamier—so try not to make more than you'll need for about a week at a time. Yogurt will keep in the refrigerator for several weeks, but the bacterial content is highest and most effective within the first seven days.

YOU BLEW IT

If your yogurt doesn't form, there could be several explanations.

1. The milk was not sufficiently heated—to just below boiling—to kill existing bacteria. Your starter was overwhelmed.

2. The milk may have been too hot (above 120°F.) or too cold (below 90°F.) when the starter was added. Remember, 115°F. is optimal.

3. The starter was not mixed thoroughly into the cooled milk.

4. The milk-and-starter mixture may have been disturbed, shaken, or otherwise vibrated during incubation.

5. Either the milk or starter may have been old, which calls for a longer incubation period. Try to start with fresh ingredients.

6. If you used a dried culture, perhaps it needed more time, sometimes as much as 15 to 20 hours, at least for the first batch.

7. The milk may have been contaminated by residues of medication (penicillin, for example) that had been given to cows for disease. Although law requires milk to be withheld from sale until all traces of medication are gone, it doesn't always happen that way. The penicillin, or whatever, would naturally kill off the yogurt culture.

Don't be discouraged if your yogurt doesn't turn out right the first time. Even Julia Child has been known to throw out dinner and start all over again.

Variations on a Theme

Now that you know how to make plain yogurt from milk and starter, it's time to get fancy.

THICKENED YOGURT

½ teaspoon unflavored
  gelatin, softened in boiling
  water to make 1 cup
1 tablespoon sugar
3 cups powdered milk mixed
  with 3 cups water

1 large (13-ounce) can
  evaporated milk
2 cups tepid water
3 tablespoons yogurt

Add sugar to gelatin and water, stir, and let cool. Mix powdered milk, evaporated milk, and water together; heat to just below boiling. Cool to 115°F. Add sugar-gelatin mixture and yogurt; stir to mix thoroughly. Incubate by your favorite method. Makes about 1¾ quarts or 7−8 servings.

TO FLAVOR OR NOT TO FLAVOR

If you eat only flavored yogurt, strawberry, for instance, and never use it in cooking or baking (although, hopefully the recipes in this book will change your mind about that), you can make a flavored, Swiss-style yogurt by simply adding ½ cup pureed strawberries, or any other fruit, per quart milk. Then heat the fruit and milk to just below boiling, allow to cool to 115°F., add 1 tablespoon yogurt starter, stir well, and incubate as you like.

Instead of fruit, you can add 3 to 6 tablespoons honey to the milk just before heating, and go on from there. But adding flavorings beforehand limits your yogurt to being a dessert or snack food, and unless you know positively that that's the only way you want to use it, it's not recommended.

Alternatively, if you make unflavored yogurt, the possibilities are practically unlimited. Imagine the pleasure of tasting a nice crisp bite of apple in a spoonful of creamy fresh yogurt. Or swirling in a few spoons of fresh raspberries in season. It's an incomparable experience, and by adding fruit as you want, or need, you'll still have a supply of unflavored yogurt ready to use in cooking. If your favorite fruit is not in season, you can always use store-bought preserves, frozen or canned fruits, or whatever you've stored away yourself after harvesting your own garden. Calories do build up this way, and if you're dieting, keep in mind that ½ cup fresh strawberries is 28 calories; ½ cup frozen is 98, and 1 tablespoon strawberry preserves is 54 calories.

When commercial producers make flavored yogurt, by the way, they invariably use preserves rather than fresh fruit (which explains why the calories in flavored yogurt are so much higher than in the plain variety). They will heat the preserves to the same temperature as the cultured milk, add and stir them, and allow the whole thing to incubate in individual containers or large vats. In some cases, the preserves are first put in the bottom of each individual container, the cultured milk poured on top, and then incubation takes place.

[6]

FROZEN YOGURT

It's been called everything from the "ice-cream alternative" to "ice cream without guilt," and everyone, from New York's elegant Bloomingdale's (one of the first, as usual) to the local neighborhood pizza parlor, is selling it, you should pardon the expression, like hotcakes. Frozen-yogurt sales went up 35 percent in 1976, and they show no signs of slowing down. Just like the phenomenal Topsy, frozen yogurt just growed and growed.

Basically, frozen yogurt is just a new form of the old familiar favorite. It's whipped, frozen, and pushed out of the same kind of machine that gives you soft ice cream. You can buy it by the cone, or prepackaged and frozen solid from the ice-cream case at the supermarket. But all similarities to ice cream end here. It doesn't taste like ice cream—although many people think it's better—and it's not as fattening. Frozen yogurt has one-third to one-half fewer calories than the same amount of ice cream; in a 3½-ounce serving, the yogurt (cone included) weighs in at a mere 115 calories, ice cream at 130 (with no cone). The actual numbers may vary a bit depending on whether the yogurt is made from skim or whole milk, and what else is added to it in the way of sweeteners, preserves, or flavorings, but even 3½ ounces of regular fruit-flavored yogurt is only 120 calories.

Compared to the same amount of milk or plain yogurt, frozen yogurt is higher in calories and carbohydrates, lower in fat, and just about the same in content of vitamins and minerals. It's the flavorings and the stabilizers that add those extra calories and carbohydrates. Sugar and preserves give it a dessert-y, appealing taste; and stabilizers, usually corn syrup or gelatin, to keep the preserves in suspension, give the frozen yogurt a stiffer body and prevent it from melting while it's being eaten.

Frozen yogurt was not an instant success story. It first came to New York in 1968, but only in a very limited number of outlets. It was never given any kind of push; all efforts were being concentrated on selling regular yogurt in the supermarkets. It was shelved for a few years, and not even thought about again until Hood successfully introduced it to the Boston-Cambridge area—at a Harvard Square cafe called The Spa—in 1972. It was a smash. In the first two years on the market, Hood's sales went up 200 percent. When Dannon opened its first frozen-yogurt store in New York, three years later, sales were phenomenal—and they still are. (Dannon, Hood, and Colombo, by the way, are the major manufacturers of frozen yogurt, and chances are, wherever you buy it, you'll be eating one of those three.)

Dannon's frozen-yogurt product, Danny-Yo, is made by first pureeing the fruit preserves so that chunks of whole fruit won't clog up the machines. Then they're mixed into the yogurt, which is liquefied and frozen for shipping. At the store, it's thawed for 36 to 48 hours, then put into the machines where it's chilled and air whipped before it's served. With some brands, the yogurt is pasteurized before it's frozen, which kills the bacteria. That hardly even matters, though, because even if the bacteria were still alive, the freezing process would finish them off. So with frozen yogurt, you get a good-tasting, maybe even low-calorie treat, but no beneficial bacterial action in your stomach.

Doing It Your Way

Which all leads us to the interesting question of whether or not you can make frozen yogurt at home. The commercial producers claim there's no way. Of course, unless you have a soft-serve ice-cream machine in your kitchen, you won't be able to get it to swirl prettily into a cone or a cup. But, in fact, you *can* produce a just-as-delicious version in your own kitchen, either using an ice-cream maker, or just your own freezer.

WITH AN ICE-CREAM MAKER

To 1 pint (16 ounces) whole-milk yogurt, add ¼ cup corn syrup, about ½ cup fresh, pureed fruit (more if you like), and mix well. Chill in the refrigerator for 2 hours, and then freeze in your ice-cream maker per the manufacturer's directions. You can use either flavored or plain yogurt as a base, and add as much or as little additional fruit as you like.

An alternative method is to make a batch of whole-milk yogurt. To it, add ½ cup evaporated milk, scalded (stir constantly when heating so no skin forms on top) and then cooled, to which has been added ½ cup sugar and 1 envelope unflavored gelatin dissolved in ¼ cup water, plus a dash of salt. Now stir in your flavoring, ½ cup, or more, fresh, pureed fruit. Chill in the refrigerator for 2 hours. Then freeze in the ice-cream maker, according to directions.

WITHOUT AN ICE-CREAM MAKER

Over low heat, dissolve 1 envelope unflavored gelatin in ¼ cup cold water, stirring constantly for about 3 minutes. Add ⅓ cup sugar and a dash of salt, give it a stir, and let it cool, off the heat. Stir in 1 cup fresh fruit (pureed in the blender), 1 cup yogurt, and 1 tablespoon lemon juice. Pour into an ice-cube tray (without the cube dividers), and freeze until firm, about 2 hours. Remove from the freezer and scrape it into a large bowl. Fold in 2 egg whites, beaten

stiff but not dry with an electric mixer until light and fluffy. Refreeze, either in the same bowl, an ice-cube tray, or individual containers, until firm, about 2 hours longer. Let it sit at room temperature for about 10 minutes to soften before serving. (If you don't want to serve the frozen yogurt at this point, keep it in the freezer, but give it enough time to soften before you do.)

Almost any fresh fruit will do; whatever is in season will be especially fine. If fresh fruit is impossible to find, unsweetened frozen fruit is second best. If you'd rather use honey than sugar, go right ahead; the proportions might change a little, but you'll have to taste-test to make sure. Let your imagination run away with you. If you've always wondered what cantaloupe yogurt tastes like, this is your golden opportunity.

[7]

COOKING WITH YOGURT

Imagine a light but richly dark chocolate cake with yogurt as the main ingredient; or a delectable chicken paprikash made with lots of paprika, chicken, onions, and tart, tangy yogurt. It isn't difficult to be a gourmet cook and still watch calories, when you reach for yogurt instead of sour cream or milk to give that extra fillip to your recipes. (One cup of low-fat yogurt is 120 calories; milk, 165; sour cream, 454; heavy cream, 838.) All you need to know are a few quick tricks to make everything go smoothly.

· Always refrigerate yogurt. It will keep several weeks in tightly covered jars, at about 40°F. The flavor gets tarter as it ages, so for really sweet-tasting yogurt, use it as soon as it's made.

· Before adding yogurt to any recipe, let it warm to room temperature. Then stir lightly with a fork for about 30 seconds, and fold into the rest of the ingredients. This will help prevent curdling when a yogurt mixture is heated.

· Try to use yogurt, when possible, at low temperatures and for short heating times. It works best, for example, when stirred into a sauce just before it's removed from the heat. If you must use it at the beginning of a recipe, mix it with a little flour, cornstarch, or arrowroot, dissolved in a little water, to prevent separating. When you're baking, there's no need to do this—flour is already in your recipe. But, as you know, temperatures above 120°F. will kill the bacilli in yogurt. Whatever you're cooking will still taste delicious, but that beneficial-bacteria aspect of using yogurt will be lost.

· Don't beat yogurt vigorously. The texture will break down. If it seems to have thinned out from mixing too much, refrigerate yogurt for about 30 minutes to restore the thickness. If, for some recipes, you want a stiffer yogurt, mix it with a beaten egg white and fold gently into the other ingredients.

· For salad dressing, use half yogurt, half mayonnaise. Yogurt has about 10 calories per tablespoon, mayonnaise 10 times as many (or, 120 calories per cup compared to 1,616). The result will be outstanding, the calories much lower.

· When substituting yogurt for milk or sour cream in baking, add one-half teaspoon baking soda per cup yogurt. When substituting it for buttermilk, thin with a little water.

· Yogurt thins out with cooking, so remember to add a little arrowroot, cornstarch, or flour, dissolved in cold water, to keep it thickened.

· If yogurt is too tart to eat plain, use it in recipes with sweet or spicy flavorings. For example, sauté a little garlic in butter, add it to the yogurt, and presto, a deliciously different sauce for pasta. Or add a little sugar to sweeten it up—about a teaspoon per cup.

· Add yogurt to pan drippings for gravy; use it to replace cream or milk in a soufflé, omelette, or quiche; use it instead of milk to give new taste to pancakes and waffles.

Try some of the recipes in this chapter. We present them to give you some ideas and get you started cooking with yogurt. Be creative. Make up your own recipes—it just takes a little imagination and a little yogurt.

Hors d'oeuvres

EGGPLANT-YOGURT APPETIZER

1 eggplant, about 1 pound
1 small onion, finely minced
1 clove garlic, finely minced
1 tablespoon fresh dill, finely
   chopped
1 teaspoon lemon juice

1 cup plain yogurt, low fat or
   regular
Salt and pepper to taste
3 tablespoons butter,
   margarine, or olive oil
1 large onion, sliced thin

Preheat oven to 350°F.

Bake eggplant, on sheet of aluminum foil, for about 1 hour, or until inside is soft and skin has collapsed. Cool.

Scrape insides of eggplant into a large bowl, and mash with a fork or beat with electric mixer at medium speed. Add minced onion, garlic, dill, lemon juice, and yogurt; blend well. Add salt and pepper to taste. Chill thoroughly.

About 30 minutes before serving, melt butter, margarine, or oil, and sauté onion slices until lightly browned. Spoon on top of chilled eggplant-yogurt mixture. Serves 4 to 6.

ARTICHOKE AND CHEESE APPETIZERS

1 small onion, finely chopped
1 clove garlic, finely minced
Oil
4 eggs
1 can (14 ounces) artichoke
   hearts
¼ cup bread crumbs,
   unseasoned
½ pound grated Cheddar
   cheese

½ cup plain yogurt, low fat or
   regular
2 tablespoons parsley, finely
   chopped
Salt and pepper to taste
Dash Worcestershire sauce

Sauté onion and garlic in oil in skillet, until soft. Beat eggs well in a large bowl. Drain artichokes and dice. Combine with eggs, and add cooked onion and garlic, bread crumbs, cheese, yogurt, parsley, salt, pepper, and Worcestershire sauce.

Pour mixture into a buttered baking dish, about 7 by 11 inches. Bake for about 30 minutes in preheated 325°F. oven.

When appetizers are done, a knife inserted in the middle will come out clean. Allow to cool slightly, and then cut into squares to serve. Makes about 15 squares.

CHAMPIGNONS ÉLÉGANTS

¼ cup butter
2 teaspoons lemon juice
2 tablespoons chopped
   parsley
Salt and pepper to taste
Toast
1 pound small mushrooms,
   the caps only

½ cup plain yogurt, low fat or
   regular
2 tablespoons sherry
Grated Parmesan cheese
   (optional)

Whip the butter with the lemon juice, parsley, salt, and pepper. Break up enough toast to cover the bottom of four individual serving dishes that are ovenproof. Use half the butter mixture to spread on the toast. Then cover the toast with the mushroom caps. Cover the caps with the rest of the butter.

Mix the yogurt with the sherry, and top each dish with a dollop of the yogurt and sherry mixture. If desired, sprinkle some grated Parmesan cheese on each dish.

Bake 30 minutes in a 350°F. oven. Serve hot. Serves 4.

CHEDDAR-YOGURT FONDUE

1 large clove garlic
1 cup plain yogurt, low fat or
   regular
1 pound Cheddar cheese,
   grated

3 or 4 tablespoons white
   wine
Fresh ground pepper to taste
Bread cubes

Rub a fondue pot or earthenware dish with cut garlic clove. Add the yogurt and heat, on top of stove, until hot, but do not boil. Add the cheese and stir frequently until the cheese is thoroughly melted. When the cheese is melted, add the wine, stirring again. Add the pepper.

Remove the pot from the stove and place over an alcohol burner with a low flame. The fondue should be hot and creamy, but not boiling.

Serve with bread cubes to dip into the fondue. Serves 4 to 6.

PIQUANT CHILI DIP

½ cup chili sauce
1 cup plain yogurt, low fat or
regular
Dash of Worcestershire sauce

Salt and pepper to taste
Dash garlic powder
Chopped green onions

Blend all ingredients well. Chill for about 30 minutes to thicken. Use with crackers or chips or raw vegetables. Serves 4 to 6.

Soups

BLENDER-EASY BEEF AND YOGURT SOUP

1½ quarts beef stock
3 tablespoons oil
¼ cup flour
2 tablespoons fresh mint or 1
tablespoon dried mint

2 cups plain yogurt, low fat or
regular
3 tablespoons brewer's yeast
(optional)

Blend everything in a blender, at medium speed, until smooth (you may have to do this in batches). Heat over low flame until thoroughly warm. Serves 8.

COLD ZUCCHINI (OR CUCUMBER) AND YOGURT SOUP

1 medium zucchini or
cucumber, coarsely chopped
1 medium onion, chopped
1 clove garlic, minced
Oil
1½ teaspoons curry powder

3 cups chicken broth
1½ cups plain yogurt, low fat
or regular
Salt and pepper to taste
Fresh parsley or dill

Sauté zucchini or cucumber, onion, and garlic, in a little oil, till tender. Sprinkle with curry powder. Put mixture in heavy saucepan, add chicken broth, and let simmer about 30 minutes, covered.

Pour the mixture into a blender (scraping pan if necessary with a rubber spatula), and puree. Add yogurt, salt, and pepper, and blend thoroughly. Chill for several hours before serving; garnish with fresh parsley or dill. Serves 4.

FROSTY FRUIT SOUP

1 stick cinnamon
3 cups water
⅔ cup sugar
2 cans (16 ounces each)
  pitted sour cherries, drained,
  and liquid reserved

2 tablespoons cornstarch
2 cups plain yogurt, low fat or
  regular
½ cup dry red wine

In a saucepan, combine cinnamon stick, water, and sugar; bring to a boil. Simmer, with pot covered partially, for about 15 minutes.

Add cornstarch to cherry liquid; stir to dissolve. Remove cinnamon stick from sugar-water syrup, and off heat, add cherry liquid, stirring with a wire whisk. Return pot to heat; stir over low heat until thickened, about five minutes.

Remove from heat. Add yogurt and wine, and cherries. Pour into large glass bowl or jar, and chill several hours before serving. Serves 4 to 6.

YOGURT-BARLEY SOUP

1 cup raw barley
2 eggs
1 tablespoon flour
1 cup plain yogurt, low fat or
  regular

2 cups cold water
2 tablespoons chopped
  onion
Salt and pepper to taste
Chopped dill or parsley

Cook the raw barley. Drain. Beat the eggs and add the flour to them, blending well. Combine the yogurt with the cold water. Blend the yogurt mixture with the egg mixture. Add the barley, onion, salt, and pepper. Cook until thick, almost to the boiling point.

This should be served ice cold, but it is also good warm. Sprinkle serving dishes of soup with chopped dill or parsley. Serves 4.

Salads

WALDORF SALAD

1 cup diced pears
1 cup diced apples
1 cup plain yogurt, low fat or
  regular
½ cup chopped walnuts

½ cup raisins
1 cup sliced celery
2 tablespoons honey
Lettuce leaves

Combine all ingredients, tossing them until fruit and nuts are well coated. Serve on lettuce leaves. Serves 2.

CUCUMBER-YOGURT SALAD

*1 small cucumber, finely
  diced
1 small onion, grated
Salt and pepper to taste*

*Fresh mint leaves, chopped
  to make ¼ cup
1 cup plain yogurt, low fat or
  regular*

Mix all ingredients well and let chill several hours before serving.
Serves 2.

POTATO SALAD

*4 medium-size boiled
  potatoes
½ teaspoon salt
¼ teaspoon dry mustard
2 teaspoons fresh parsley,
  minced*

*Dash pepper
2 tablespoons vinegar
1 cup plain yogurt, low fat or
  regular
Paprika
1 teaspoon sugar*

Peel and thinly slice potatoes. Mix the rest of the ingredients together, with the exception of the yogurt and paprika. Then add the
yogurt and blend well. Pour over the sliced potatoes, and toss so that
all are covered with the dressing.
  Garnish with paprika for coloring. This may be served warm or
cold. Serves 2 to 3.

TURKEY SALAD

*3 cups diced cooked turkey
½ cup plain yogurt, low fat or
  regular
3 tablespoons salad oil
1 teaspoon salt*

*½ cup celery, sliced
½ cup green pepper, diced
1 teaspoon grated onion
Lettuce leaves*

Combine all ingredients, mixing well so that dressing covers all.
Serve cold on lettuce leaves. Serves 4.

Dressings

SWEET YOGURT DRESSING

¼ cup wine vinegar
Salt and freshly ground
    pepper to taste
¾ cup light salad oil
    (approximate)
½ cup plain yogurt, low fat or
    regular

2 teaspoons honey
1 tablespoon wheat germ
¼ cup golden raisins
    (optional)

In a blender, mix vinegar with salt and pepper. Slowly add oil, with blender at low speed, till all mixed in. Add yogurt, honey, and wheat germ; blend thoroughly. For a sweeter dressing, or to use over fruit, add raisins before serving. Yield: 1½ cups.

GARLIC AND YOGURT DRESSING

1 or 2 cloves garlic, chopped
2 tablespoons fresh parsley,
    chopped, or 1 tablespoon
    dried parsley
1 tablespoon chives,
    chopped
1 teaspoon lemon juice or
    vinegar

½ teaspoon lemon rind,
    grated
Salt and freshly ground
    pepper to taste
1 cup plain yogurt, low fat or
    regular

Put all ingredients in a blender and blend at high speed until smooth. Yield: 1 cup.

YOGURT AND COTTAGE CHEESE DRESSING

1 cup plain yogurt, low fat or
    regular
1 cup cottage cheese, low fat
    preferably
½ teaspoon dill
¼ teaspoon poppy seeds
Salt and pepper to taste

2 tablespoons chives,
    chopped
1 small cucumber, finely
    diced
6 radishes, chopped
½ tablespoon salad oil

Blend yogurt and cottage cheese in a blender until smooth. Add rest of ingredients and blend well. Yield: 1 cup.

Seafood

WELLFLEET SOLE

1 pound fillet of sole
1 large green pepper, sliced
1 sliced tomato
¼ pound mushrooms,
  chopped
1 small onion, diced

2 tablespoons butter or
  margarine
1 cup plain yogurt, low fat or
  regular
Salt and pepper to taste

Lay sole in baking dish. Cover with green pepper, tomato, mushrooms, and onion. Dot with butter or margarine. Pour yogurt over all. Season with salt and pepper. Bake 25 minutes at 350°F. Serves 2.

CRABMEAT AND SHRIMP CURRY

1 pound shrimp, cleaned and
  deveined
1 pound crabmeat, with shell
  removed
Margarine, melted
1 large onion, chopped
3 to 5 cloves garlic, finely
  minced
2 teaspoons turmeric

1 teaspoon ground ginger
4 tablespoons coriander
2 tablespoons cumin
1 teaspoon red pepper flakes
2 tablespoons chopped mint
1 to 1½ cups plain yogurt,
  low fat or regular
4 tablespoons lemon juice
Rice

Cook the shrimp and crabmeat in about 1 tablespoon melted margarine, about 3 minutes. Remove the shrimp and crabmeat, and set aside. In the same pan, adding a little more margarine if necessary, cook the onion and garlic until soft. Add the turmeric, ginger, coriander, cumin, red pepper flakes (test for hotness after adding), and mint. Cook for about 5 minutes. Add the yogurt and blend well, but do not allow to boil. Remove from heat, stir in the shrimp and crabmeat, and sprinkle with the lemon juice. Serve over rice. Serves 4.

SEAFOOD CRÊPES

CRÊPES:

2 eggs	*¼ teaspoon salt*
1 tablespoon oil	*1 teaspoon sugar*
⅔ cup milk	*Butter, melted*
½ cup sifted flour	

Beat eggs. Add oil and milk. After sifting flour with salt and sugar, add to egg mixture. Beat until smooth, but do not overbeat. Refrigerate for at least two hours or overnight. When ready to make crêpes, brush a skillet, 5 or 6 inches in diameter, with melted butter. When pan is hot, remove from stove, and add 3 tablespoons batter. Tilt the pan so that batter covers the bottom, spreading in a circle to the edges. Replace pan on the heat and cook for about a minute. Flip the crêpe over and cook the other side for half a minute. Crêpes should be stacked between wax paper. Makes 8–10 crêpes.

FILLING:

Butter, melted	*3 tablespoons flour*
½ cup sliced mushrooms	*1 egg yolk*
¼ cup diced green pepper	*1 cup plain yogurt, low fat or*
1 pound crabmeat	*regular*
3 tablespoons sherry	

Melt a few tablespoons butter in a saucepan. Add the mushrooms and sauté until brown. Then remove the mushrooms and add the green pepper, cooking until soft. Remove the green pepper, and add the crabmeat to the pan, adding more butter when necessary. Sprinkle the sherry over the crabmeat and cook for 5 minutes. Blend in the green pepper and the mushrooms.

Add the flour and blend thoroughly. Beat the egg yolk and add to the yogurt. Blend the yogurt and egg mixture into the crabmeat, and allow the filling to thicken.

Fill each crêpe with a few (2 or 3) teaspoons filling. This dish may be frozen and then reheated in the oven, if desired. Should fill eight crêpes.

Chicken

CHICKEN SAHIB

3-pound chicken, quartered
4 cups plain yogurt, low fat or
   regular
1 cup rice, uncooked
1 medium onion, chopped
1 or 2 cloves garlic, minced

2 tablespoons curry powder
½ teaspoon ginger
4 tablespoons apricot
   preserves
¼ cup golden raisins
Salt and pepper to taste

Place chicken in a casserole or roaster. Mix the rest of the ingredients together and pour over chicken, turning pieces to coat well. Let sit for a couple of hours, turning two or three times.

Preheat oven to 350°F.

Cover casserole or roaster tightly with aluminum foil; pierce with fork, to let steam escape. Bake for 1 hour or until chicken is tender. Serves 4.

TANDOORI CHICKEN

2½- or 3-pound chicken, cut
   into serving pieces, or an
   equal amount of your
   favorite chicken parts
1 cup plain yogurt, low fat or
   regular
⅓ cup lime juice
3 cloves garlic, finely
   chopped
2 teaspoons fresh ginger
   root, grated

2 teaspoons coriander
1 teaspoon salt
1½ teaspoon paprika
½ teaspoon cayenne
1 teaspoon cumin
½ teaspoon ground anise
   seeds (optional)
⅓ cup butter, melted
2 limes, cut into wedges

Wash chicken; pat dry with paper towels; set aside.

In a large bowl, combine all ingredients except chicken, butter, and limes; mix well. Add chicken pieces; stir to coat with marinade. Cover bowl with plastic wrap or aluminum foil and marinate in refrigerator at least 24 hours, turning frequently.

Preheat oven to 375°F.

Place chicken and marinade in roasting pan. Bake for 45 to 60 minutes, or until chicken is done; baste several times with melted butter. Serve garnished with lime wedges. Serves 4.

ROAST CHICKEN WITH YOGURT

3- or 4-pound chicken
2 tablespoons ginger,
   chopped fine
1 medium onion, chopped
   fine

1 cup plain yogurt, low fat
   or regular
1 teaspoon salt
Freshly ground black pepper

Prick skin of chicken all over with two-prong fork. Combine ginger, onion, yogurt, salt, and pepper. Rub mixture into chicken. Marinate in covered bowl or plastic bag for several hours or overnight.

Preheat oven to 350°F.

Place chicken and marinade in roasting pan, and roast for 1 to 1½ hours, or until leg joint moves easily. Remove from pan. Scrape up juices by adding a little boiling water or white wine, and pour over chicken. Serves 4.

TARRAGON-YOGURT CHICKEN

3-pound chicken, cut into
   serving pieces, or an
   equal amount of boned,
   skinned chicken breasts
1 cup dry white wine
1 cup chicken broth
2 tablespoons tarragon
Salt and pepper to taste

1 cup plain yogurt, low fat
   or regular, mixed with 1
   tablespoon flour, or
   cornstarch dissolved in a
   little water
2 teaspoons butter
2 teaspoons flour

Place chicken, in one layer, in a heavy casserole. Add the wine, chicken broth, tarragon, and salt and pepper. Bring to a boil and cook about 15 to 20 minutes if you are using just the breasts; about 25 to 30 minutes if the whole chicken.

Take the chicken out of the pot and keep warm. Reduce the sauce to half over a high heat. Add the yogurt mixture and cook 8 to 10 minutes (the cornstarch or flour should keep it from separating). Taste and correct seasonings. Still over heat, add the butter and flour, which have been blended together into a paste, and stir until thickened. Pour sauce over chicken. Serves 4.

Beef

YOGURT-BEEF KABOBS

1½ pounds lean beef, cubed
1 cup plain yogurt, low fat or
  regular
1 teaspoon salt
½ teaspoon freshly ground
  black pepper

2 cloves garlic, minced
¼ cup lemon juice
2 teaspoons cumin

Place beef cubes in a large bowl. Combine yogurt with rest of ingredients; pour over meat. Stir to coat well. Refrigerate, covered, several hours or overnight.

Preheat broiler. Put beef on skewers and broil, about 5 to 7 inches from flame, for a total of about 15 minutes; turn once or twice. Brush with remaining marinade while broiling. Serves 2.

SWEDISH MEATBALLS

Margarine, melted
1 small onion, minced
1 egg
½ cup milk
½ cup fresh bread crumbs
2 teaspoons salt
½ teaspoon allspice

¼ teaspoon nutmeg
1 pound ground chuck
⅛ teaspoon pepper
3 tablespoons flour
1 cup plain yogurt, low fat or
  regular

Sauté minced onion, in a small amount of margarine in skillet, until soft. Beat egg in mixing bowl. Combine with milk and bread crumbs. Allow to remain for 10 minutes. Then add salt, allspice, nutmeg, chuck, onion, and pepper.

Shape into small balls, about ¾ inch in diameter. Sauté balls in skillet with margarine, browning well on all sides. Remove balls when done, to make room for more.

After all meatballs are cooked, make gravy in drippings in skillet. Stir in flour, and add yogurt, cooking until thick. Replace balls in skillet and heat mixture through. Serves 2.

Veal and Lamb

VEAL WITH YOGURT-DILL SAUCE

Oil
4 pounds stewing veal, cut
* into cubes*
5 cups water
2 carrots, chopped
1 stalk celery, chopped
1 bay leaf
5 peppercorns
Salt

3 tablespoons butter
1 cup chopped onions
3 tablespoons flour
1 teaspoon sugar
3 teaspoons lemon juice
3 tablespoons chopped dill
1 cup plain yogurt, low fat or
* regular*

Sauté the veal in a few tablespoons oil in a large Dutch oven. Add the water, carrots, celery, bay leaf, peppercorns, and salt. Cover and simmer until the veal is tender, about 1 to 2 hours.

Remove the veal and strain the stock. Boil the stock down until only 2 cups of liquid are left.

Melt the butter and cook the chopped onions until soft but not brown. Add the flour and blend well. Add the stock gradually, until the mixture is combined thoroughly. When thickened, add the sugar, lemon juice, and dill. Cook about 10 to 15 minutes more, stirring frequently.

Remove from heat and add the yogurt. Add the veal and heat again, if necessary, to serving temperature. If desired, you may also add the chopped celery and carrots to the sauce at this time. Serves 8.

LEG OF LAMB MARINATED IN YOGURT

1 cup plain yogurt, low fat or
* regular*
¼ cup oil, olive or light salad

½ cup onion, grated
Salt and pepper to taste
6- or 7-pound leg of lamb

In a large plastic bag, mix yogurt, oil, onion, and salt and pepper. Add lamb; seal bag tightly. With your hands, through the bag, spread the marinade over the lamb. Place in the refrigerator overnight, or leave at room temperature for 6 to 8 hours, turning every now and then to spread marinade evenly.

Preheat oven to 500°F.

In a roasting pan a bit larger than the lamb, place meat (after having removed it from the bag). Squeeze the remaining marinade out of the bag and over the leg. Bake, without covering, until it is very well browned, between 30 to 40 minutes. To keep the meat from sticking to the pan, add between ½ to 1 cup water, and make sure there is always at least ¼ cup liquid on the bottom of the pan.

When meat has browned, turn it to one side and bake for an additional 15 minutes. Cover with lid of roaster or aluminum foil, reduce heat to 375°F., and continue baking for 1 to 1½ hours, or until tender.

Skim fat from juices in pan; discard. Serve lamb with natural pan gravy on the side.

Serves four big eaters, six smaller ones.

Vegetables

YOGURT-VEGETABLE MEDLEY

Oil
3 cups zucchini, sliced
3 cups eggplant, cubed
½ cup diced onion
1 can (one pound)
* tomatoes, chopped*
½ teaspoon salt
½ teaspoon pepper
½ cup plain yogurt, low fat
* or regular*
¾ pound feta cheese,
* crumbled*
Chopped dill or mint
* (optional)*

Sauté zucchini, eggplant, and onion in a few teaspoons oil in a frying pan. After about 5 minutes, add tomatoes, salt, and pepper. Cover and cook for about 15 minutes. Stir in the yogurt, and heat another 3 to 5 minutes.

Remove from stove and add feta cheese on top. If desired, also add some chopped dill or mint to taste. Serves 6.

This may also be used as a sauce for pasta.

MUSHROOM CURRY

1 pound fresh mushrooms
4 tablespoons butter
1 medium onion, chopped
 fine
1 tablespoon curry powder

1 medium apple, chopped
Salt and pepper to taste
2½ cups plain yogurt, low
 fat or regular
½ teaspoon paprika

Leave caps of mushrooms whole and chop the stems. Melt butter in skillet; sauté mushroom caps until they are just lightly browned and have absorbed most of the butter, about 5 minutes. Remove to small bowl and set aside.

Add onion and curry powder to pan and sauté until onion is transparent (add more butter if necessary). Add the chopped apple, chopped mushroom stems, and salt and pepper. Cook a little while longer, until mushrooms are tender.

Remove from heat; stir in yogurt and paprika. Return to heat to warm, and add mushroom caps. Serve over rice. Serves 4.

SPINACH-NOODLE CASSEROLE

3 cups egg noodles, cooked
 and drained
7½ tablespoons butter,
 melted
1 teaspoon salt
½ cup grated Swiss cheese
¼ cup grated Parmesan
 cheese
1 cup plain yogurt, low fat or
 regular

1 cup onions, finely
 chopped
3 cups cooked spinach,
 chopped and drained
Pepper to taste
½ cup bread crumbs,
 unseasoned

Preheat oven to 350°F.

Mix noodles, 1½ tablespoons melted butter, and half the salt together in a large bowl, and set aside. In a separate bowl, mix all but about ¼ cup of the combined grated cheeses with the yogurt. Beat well.

Melt 3 tablespoons butter in a skillet. Add onions and cook until soft. Add spinach, and cook over high heat until all the moisture has been evaporated, and spinach is starting to stick to pan. Add the rest of the salt, and the pepper. Melt 2 tablespoons butter in a skillet. Remove from heat and add the bread crumbs and the ¼ cup leftover cheese.

Grease bottom and sides of a 1½- or 2-quart baking dish with rest of butter. Put a layer of noodles on the bottom, top with half the spinach, and half the yogurt and cheese mixture. Repeat once more, ending with noodles. Sprinkle with the bread crumbs and cheese, dot with additional butter, and bake for 30 minutes until topping is brown. Serves 4–6.

Breads

PEANUT BUTTER-YOGURT BREAD

4 teaspoons baking powder
1 teaspoon salt
2 cups flour
1 tablespoon wheat germ

1¼ cups plain yogurt, low
   fat or regular
⅔ cup peanut butter
⅛ cup honey

Preheat oven to 350°F.

Sift dry ingredients together in large bowl. Mix in wheat germ.

In a separate bowl, thoroughly mix together remaining ingredients until smooth. Combine with sifted mixture until well blended, and pour or scrape into greased 8½-by-4½-inch loaf pan.

Bake about 50 minutes, or until done. Cool on rack, out of pan.

This is better the next day, but it's certainly delicious just cooled from the oven. Makes 1 loaf.

BANANA-BOSTON BROWN BREAD

2 cups yogurt, low fat or
   regular
¾ cup molasses
¾ cup raisins
2 tablespoons oil

1 cup ripe bananas, mashed
2 cups whole wheat flour
1 cup cornmeal
1 teaspoon baking soda
1 teaspoon salt

Preheat oven to 350°F.

Combine yogurt, molasses, raisins, oil, and bananas. Set aside.

In a large bowl, mix together dry ingredients; stir in the yogurt mixture.

Grease three 1-pound coffee cans, and lightly dust them with flour. Spoon batter into them, filling about one-half to two-thirds full. Bake for about 1 hour or until toothpick inserted in center comes out clean. Cool before serving, but serve while still warm. Makes three loaves.

HEALTH MUFFINS

1 cup whole wheat flour
1 teaspoon salt
1 tablespoon baking powder
¼ cup instant nonfat dry
  milk
1 cup bran flakes
1 cup wheat germ
1 cup plain yogurt, low fat or
  regular

2 eggs, beaten
¼ cup honey
1 tablespoon grated orange
  rind
2 tablespoons safflower oil
½ cup raisins
½ cup chopped walnuts

Mix flour, salt, baking powder, and milk in mixing bowl. Add rest of the ingredients and stir just enough to moisten thoroughly. Spoon the mixture into well-greased muffin tins, filling almost two-thirds full.

Bake in a preheated 400°F. oven for about 15 to 20 minutes, until tops of muffins are brown. Makes 12 muffins.

YOGURT-GRANOLA BREAD

2 cups whole wheat flour
2 packages active dry yeast
½ cup wheat germ
2 tablespoons sesame seeds,
  toasted
2 teaspoons salt
1 cup fruit-and-nut granola
1½ cups water
1 cup plain yogurt, low fat or
  regular

2 tablespoons butter or
  margarine
½ cup orange or lemon
  marmalade, or apricot
  preserves
¼ cup molasses
4 to 6 cups flour
1 egg

Mix whole wheat flour, yeast, wheat germ, sesame seeds, salt, and granola together in a large bowl. Set aside.

Over low heat, heat water, yogurt, butter or margarine, marmalade or preserves, and molasses, until about 120°F. to 130°F. Add gradually to dry mixture, then beat with electric mixer at medium speed for two minutes. Start with 4 cups, and gradually add enough flour, stirring constantly, to make a soft dough.

Turn out onto lightly floured board; knead about 10 minutes until smooth and elastic. Place in greased bowl, turning to grease top. Cover and let rise in warm place, until doubled in bulk, about 1 hour.

Punch down; remove from bowl. Divide in two and form into balls, or place in oiled and lightly floured bread pans. Cover, let rise until doubled in bulk in warm place, about 1 hour.

Preheat oven to 375°F.

Slash the tops of the loaves with a sharp knife. Beat the egg with 1 tablespoon water, and brush over loaves. Bake about 45 minutes, or until breads sound hollow when tapped. If they start to brown too quickly, cover with aluminum foil. Makes 2 loaves.

Desserts

DEEP SOUTH GLAZED ORANGE-YOGURT CAKE

CAKE:

1 cup (two sticks) butter or
  margarine, softened
1 cup sugar
3 eggs, separated
1 teaspoon baking powder
1 teaspoon baking soda

2 cups flour
1 cup plain yogurt, low fat or
  regular
2 tablespoons orange peel,
  finely grated

GLAZE:

¼ cup orange juice
¼ cup orange rind,
  grated coarsely

½ cup sugar
½ cup orange liqueur

Preheat oven to 350°F.

Grease, and lightly dust with flour, a 9-inch tube or Bundt pan. Set aside.

Cream butter and sugar together, until light and fluffy, with electric mixer on medium speed. Separately, beat egg yolks until frothy. Add to butter-sugar mixture and blend thoroughly. Again in another bowl, sift together dry ingredients and add alternately with yogurt to the butter, eggs, and sugar mixture. Mix gently but thoroughly, and add orange rind. Beat egg whites until stiff but not dry, and lightly fold into rest of batter.

Pour into pan; bake for 40 minutes, or until knife or toothpick inserted comes out clean. Cool in pan for 10 minutes; invert on wire rack.

To make glaze, combine orange juice, rind, liqueur, and sugar. Bring to a boil for 2 minutes.

Glaze with syrup while cake is still warm.

YOGURT CHEESECAKE

CRUST:

¼ cup wheat germ
1 teaspoon cinnamon
or

6 ounces zweiback
¼ cup sugar
¼ cup butter or margarine,
melted

FILLING:

8 eggs, at room
temperature
4 cups (about 2 pounds)
cottage cheese
3 tablespoons lemon juice
1 teaspoon grated lemon
rind

1 cup plain yogurt, low fat or
regular
1 cup honey
¼ cup flour, sifted

GLAZE:

½ cup crushed strawberries
⅓ cup sugar
¼ cup water

1 tablespoon cornstarch
1 teaspoon butter
Whole strawberries

Preheat oven to 350°F.

Grease well a 9-inch springform pan. Mix wheat germ and cinnamon, and sprinkle pan with mixture.

Or crush zweiback into fine crumbs and roll in greased pan until evenly coated. Mix whatever is left of zweiback crumbs with sugar and melted butter and press onto the bottom of the pan. Bake for 5 minutes until set; let cool.

Beat the eggs with an electric mixer until very thick and lemon colored. Add the cottage cheese, a little at a time, and beat well—until smooth—after each addition. Stir in the rest of the ingredients. Mix well, until smooth and creamy.

Pour into pan; bake for 1 hour. Then, turn off oven but leave cake in for additional 1½ hours. *Do not open oven door.* Chill overnight.

One hour before serving, cheesecake can be glazed. To make glaze, blend strawberries, sugar, water, and cornstarch, and bring to a boil for 2 minutes. Add butter, mix well, and strain. Place whole strawberries on top of cake and pour glaze over all. Chill for about 1 hour.

SPICY YOGURT CAKE

2 cups sugar
1 cup (2 sticks) butter, at
  room temperature
2¼ cups flour
1 cup plain yogurt, low fat or
  regular
3 eggs

1 teaspoon vanilla
½ teaspoon salt
½ teaspoon baking soda
¼ teaspoon ground cloves
1 teaspoon cinnamon
1 teaspoon allspice
½ teaspoon nutmeg

Preheat oven to 325°F.

Grease, and lightly dust with flour, a 10-inch Bundt or tube pan. Set aside.

With an electric mixer set at medium, cream butter and sugar well until light and fluffy. Stir in remaining ingredients. Beat well, at low speed, until thoroughly mixed; scrape bowl often with a rubber spatula to make sure all ingredients are combined. Beat 4 minutes longer at high speed, again, scraping bowl.

Pour into pan. Bake 1 hour or until knife or toothpick inserted comes out clean. Place on wire rack and cool 10 minutes. Remove from pan; leave on rack till completely cooled.

NO-BAKE YOGURT-CREAM CHEESE PIE

CRUST:

½ cup rolled oats or
  chopped almonds
½ cup chopped, pitted dates
1 to 2 tablespoons butter,
  melted

or
1 sweet 8-inch
  graham-cracker crust

FILLING:

1 cup plain yogurt, low fat or
  regular
1 8-ounce package cream
  cheese, softened
1 tablespoon honey

1 tablespoon vanilla
½ cup (approximate) sliced
  fresh fruit or berries in
  season, or well-drained
  frozen or canned fruit

Combine the oats (or almonds) and dates. Mix thoroughly with the melted butter and press into an 8-inch pie plate. Or use your favorite sweet graham-cracker crust. Chill.

In a large bowl, with electric mixer set at medium, or by hand, beat yogurt, cream cheese, honey, and vanilla till well blended and very smooth. Spread fruit on bottom of pie crust; pour yogurt mixture over fruit. Chill several hours or overnight until set.

SILKEN YOGURT PUDDING

*4 cups yogurt, drained
   overnight through
   cheesecloth or a fine sieve
1 cup sugar
½ teaspoon nutmeg
¼ teaspoon saffron threads,
   crumbled*

*1 teaspoon rose water
   (available in drugstores)
Ground seed from 1
   cardamon pod*

Cover the top of a large mixing bowl very tightly with a piece of muslin. Fasten it securely with two or three heavy rubber bands so it won't pull out or move around.

Put 2 cups yogurt and ½ cup sugar on top of the muslin, and using your hands, push it through into the bowl. When through, do the same with the remaining yogurt and sugar. (This is what gives the pudding its silky texture.)

When all the sugar and yogurt have been used up, remove the muslin, scrape the underside, and mix in the rest of the ingredients. Stir well; chill before serving. Serves 6 to 8.

YOGURT PUDDING

*2 cups yogurt, drained
   overnight through
   cheesecloth
4 tablespoons sugar*

*Pistachio nuts, about one
   ounce, chopped
½ teaspoon ground
   cardamon*

When the yogurt has drained, add the sugar. Whip to give a creamy texture. Add pistachio nuts to top of pudding or else blend with the body of the pudding, however desired. Blend in the ground cardamon and serve well chilled. Serves 4.

Beverages

LASSI (An Indian Yogurt Beverage)

1 cup plain yogurt, low fat or
　regular
1 cup fresh fruit juice
　(pineapple, apple, apricot,
　etc.)

2 bananas
¼ teaspoon cinnamon or
　nutmeg
Honey or sugar to taste
Ice

Put all ingredients in a blender set at medium to high speed; blend until smooth, and ice is crushed. The more ice you add, the thinner it will be. Serves 2.

SPICY LASSI

1 quart cold water
1 cup yogurt
Dash salt and cayenne
　pepper

½ teaspoon ground cumin
　seed, roasted

In a large bowl, mix the water and yogurt with a rotary beater or a wire whisk. Add the rest of the ingredients and stir well. Chill for several hours before serving. Serves 4.

YOGURT JULEP

1 cup plain yogurt
½ cup cold water
1 teaspoon chopped fresh
　mint, or to taste

Dash salt

Blend all ingredients till smooth in a blender, or beat in a large bowl with a wire whisk. Pour over ice. Serves 2.

PINEAPPLE-ORANGE YOGURT SHAKE*

1 6-ounce can frozen
   orange-juice concentrate
1 cup crushed pineapple
2 cups plain yogurt, low fat
   or regular

2 eggs
1 cup instant nonfat dry milk
2 tablespoons honey

At high speed, combine all ingredients in a blender until smooth; scrape down sides with a spatula if necessary. Chill or serve over ice. Serves 2 to 4.

*Instead of orange-juice concentrate, try pineapple or pineapple-orange, or for a little tarter taste, grapefruit-pineapple or grapefruit-orange. Also try substituting fresh or frozen strawberries, raspberries, or almost any fruit or fruit juice.

EASY MORNING PICK-ME-UP

1 cup plain yogurt, low fat or
   regular
2 tablespoons wheat germ
1 egg

2 tablespoons brown sugar
   or honey
2 tablespoons any frozen
   juice concentrate

Whirl all ingredients at high speed in a blender until smooth. Chill before serving. 1 serving.

FLOATY YOGURT

3 or 4 heaping tablespoons
   strawberry yogurt*
Ginger ale

1 scoop strawberry ice
   cream*

Fill a tall glass with the yogurt; add ginger ale till it's about two-thirds full; mix thoroughly. Spoon in ice cream, fill glass to top with ginger ale. 1 serving.

*Try vanilla ice cream and plain yogurt, or any fruit-flavored ice cream and yogurt combination with ginger ale, lemon, or lime soda; almost any variation you can think of will make a delicious float.

[8]

YOGURT TRIVIA

· Dannon had an ad campaign featuring a fictional yogurt-flavor inventor named Gerald, who "came from out of the pages of yogurt history" to invent the newest flavor—natural lemon. Gerald was renamed Mortimer when Ford became President.

· Ralph Nader sued Dannon for using a character named Ron Raider—a fictitious consumer advocate in their commercials. Nader claimed Raider, who endorsed Dannon, was a form of commercial exploitation without consent. They settled out of court.

· Yogurt has been called "sour milk with a college education" because people thought "cultured" meant something to do with book learning.

· There is an old joke about a ninety-seven-year-old yogurt-eating mother who died, but the baby lived.

· Yogurt is a favorite among skiers because it fits so easily into a parka pocket, and can be conveniently eaten on the slopes.

· During the 1972 U.S. Tennis Open at Forest Hills, 7,000 containers of yogurt were eaten in two weeks by the tennis pros.

· Who eats yogurt: Willis Reed, the Duchess of Windsor, Gloria Swanson, Lainie Kazan, Bob Hope, Arlene Francis, Danny Kaye, Ron Swoboda, Laurence Olivier, Burgess Meredith, Claire Bloom, Miss Lillian, Princess Grace.

· Where can you find yogurt: IBM corporate dining room, cafeteria vending machines, airline service carts, Chock full o' Nuts, the menu of the Algonquin Hotel.

· Women eat twice as much yogurt as men.

· New York and California consume more yogurt per capita than any other state.

· People who earn $15,000 or more are twice as likely to buy yogurt as those who earn under $5,000.

· Men between the ages of twenty and twenty-four eat the least amount of yogurt.

· Yogurt contains about 20 billion live bacteria in each milliliter.

· The most alcoholic of all yogurts is *busa,* a product of Turkestan. It is 7.1 percent alcohol—made so by the addition of lactose-fermenting yeasts. Similar are: Norway's *kaelder milk, urda* from the Carpathians. *skuta* from Chile, and Middle Eastern *leben.*

· The most popular flavors of yogurt are strawberry, cherry, peach, and blueberry.

· More city dwellers eat yogurt than people in suburban or rural areas.

· The perfect pH for yogurt is around 4.2.

· Whites eat more yogurt than blacks; Jews eat more yogurt than Catholics and Protestants.

[9]

YOGURT AROUND THE WORLD

Yogurt by any other name is still yogurt, whether it's called *messoradu* in Sicily and made from cow's milk, or *dahi* in India and made from the milk of water buffaloes.

Almost every country has a special kind of yogurt and its own name for it, not to mention its own favorite kind of milk, starter culture, and method for making it.

A few of the many things yogurt is called around the world and the different milks used to make it are:

- Armenia—Madzoon or Matsoon—goat's or cow's milk
- Sardinia—Gioddu—goat's or cow's milk
- Sweden—Filmjolk—cow's milk
- Denmark—Taetle—raw cow's milk; gelatinous texture
- Finland—Plimoe—skim milk
- Norway—Kaelder milk (cellar milk)—2.5% lactic acid, 0.5–1% alcohol; ropy texture is unique to Norway
- Iceland—Skyr—cow's or goat's milk
- France—Yaourt—cow's or goat's milk
- Chile—Skuta or whey champagne—cow's or goat's milk
- Burma—Tyre—cow's, goat's or buffalo's milk
- Balkans—Tarho—cow's or goat's milk
- Turkestan—Busa—water buffalo's, cow's, goat's, sheep's milk; 0.78% lactic acid, 7.1% alcohol
- Carpathians—Haslanka or Urda—cow's or goat's milk
- Greece—Oxygala—cow's or goat's milk
- Iran—Mast—cow's or goat's milk
- Lapland—Pauria—mare's milk
- Iraq, Syria, Lebanon, Israel—Leben—cow's, goat's, buffalo's, plus yeast
- Siberia, South Russia, central Asia—Koumiss or kefir—mare's milk
- Caucasus—Kuban—cow's, goat's
- Russia—Varenetz or Prostokvasha—cow's, goat's or mare's milk
- India—Dahi, Lassi, Chass, or Matta—water buffalo's, cow's, goat's, sheep's or ass's milk
- Bulgaria—Yogurt—cow's, goat's or water buffalo's milk

APPENDIX: MAIL-ORDER SOURCES FOR DRY CULTURES

Gaymont Laboratories Inc.
400 N. Orleans Street
Chicago, Ill.
60610

International Yogurt Company
628 North Doheny Drive
Los Angeles, Calif.
90069

Rosell Bacteriological Institute
La Trappe
Quebec, Canada

Dairy Laboratories
2300 Locust Street
Philadelphia, Pa.
19103

INDEX